The NEW OUTREACH

Doing Good the Better Way: An ABC Planning Guide

Sandra S. Swan

Cartoons by Jay Sidebotham

@⁄@

*To the memory of Bob Tharp,
friend and mentor,
whose spirit lives on in this book.*

@⁄@

Copyright © 2010 by Sandra S. Swan
Illustrations copyright © 2010 Jay Sidebotham

Cover illustration by Jay Sidebotham
Cover design by Christina Moore
Interior design and typesetting by MediaLynx

Swan, Sandra S.
    The new outreach : doing good the better way / Sandra S. Swan.
        p. cm.
    Includes bibliographical references and index.
    ISBN 978-0-89869-644-8 (pbk.)

 1. Church work. I. Title.
  BV4400.S88 2010
  267--dc22

                      2009044096

Church Publishing, Incorporated
445 Fifth Avenue
New York, New York 10016

www.churchpublishing.org

5 4 3 2 1

Table of Contents

Acknowledgments

My deepest thanks to my development colleagues who taught me everything I know about the better way of doing good. I especially thank my dear friends at Episcopal Relief and Development: Mary, Abagail, Brian and Janette. You have proved every day that exemplary development programs give people dignity, hope, and choices.

To those who encouraged me to write this book, and who provided so much insight, support, and ideas—I couldn't have done it without you.

To Marta, who led the way and urged me on.

And to my husband, Bruce, my very best friend.

Introduction

You have picked up this book because you are the kind of person who understands that far too many people in the world are still suffering. You know that in spite of all the well-meaning aid and outreach programs that have been carried out over the past decades, more than a billion people still live on less than one dollar a day. You have a soft spot in your heart for those who are hurting, or hungry, or homeless. A shoeless boy, or a sick baby, a struggling malnourished family—these pictures haunt you and make you uncomfortable.

You believe that every person in the world has a right to a safe and secure home, nutritious food for each member of the family, clean water, and essential health care. Those of us who have been blessed with a home, enough food, prompt medical care, and a safe environment are the lucky ones in the world. You want others to be able to share this better way of life that we enjoy. You recognize that each of us has a moral and ethical obligation to reach out to those in need. You worry that much effort has been spent, yet needs still exist. You wonder why all the aid of so many well-meaning people over the years hasn't fixed all of the ills of the world. You begin to suspect that a better way to do good must exist.

You appreciate all those who devote their time, their talents, and their money to programs of assistance. You've undoubtedly done it yourself. You know that a person need not be wealthy nor powerful to make a difference in the lives of others.

You have seen that a small act of courage and concern can reap huge rewards. You understand that a tiny gesture toward someone in need can be a huge boost toward self-sufficiency. Have you heard this story?

A young man was walking along a deserted beach in the early morning. The tide had gone out, stranding thousands of starfish above the waterline. The young man was picking up the starfish, one by one, and tossing them into the sea.

An older man was also out walking that morning. He approached the young man and pointed out, logically, that he was wasting his time—that he couldn't possibly save all the starfish. "What difference does it make?" the older man demanded.

The young man paused with a small starfish in his hand, then tossed it into the surf as he replied, "It makes a difference to this one."

Just as the young man was doing what he could to save the starfish, you have done what you can to save lives. But just as the young man recognized he couldn't save every starfish, you too grasp that you can't save everyone in need. No matter how admirable your motive has been, no matter how hard you have worked, no matter what resources you've contributed, you have been discouraged at the number of starfish still marooned on the beach.

You've been doing the best you know how, but you know people are still hurting. You've been doing good work, and good things, but you haven't always gotten the results you wanted. You have seen vast amounts of money spent on assistance programs, with little result. You begin to wonder if there isn't a better way.

And there is! That is what this book is all about—the better way of doing good. Doing good—creating a better world—is what we're aiming for here. But to do that, we need to recognize that what we have been doing, the way we have been going about it, just isn't enough. It isn't solving the problems. It is making a small difference here and there, and thank heavens for that. But we need to make a bigger and better difference. This book tells how to do just that.

This book is not written for the expert. This book is written for each one of us who has the passion and the courage to tackle those miserable conditions that are shackling persons to lives of little promise and much pain. Each one of us can have an impact, and each one of us can have a bigger impact if we approach our work in a better way. We learn a new skill by studying from those who have already achieved a degree of expertise. We can copy the best practices of those who are effective in their work. So too we can learn new ways of approaching assistance programs from those who have been running them.

Those who manage exemplary assistance programs have much to teach us. They have learned many of the secrets of an effective and efficient assistance program. They have put these secrets (actually, they are not all that secret) into practice and have the fine results to show for it.

This book reveals those secrets and makes them easy for the average person to understand and to apply. Actually, the secrets aren't even very earth-shattering; most of them are just common sense or the result of years of trial and error. What we need to do is to take advantage of everything that we know, and apply it to our charitable programs.

(By the way, in this book we will use the terms *philanthropic, charitable,* and *outreach* pretty much as synonyms. There are some minor differences that we'll point out later, but for the time being, just use whichever word you are most comfortable with.)

If you are already engaged in a philanthropic (or charitable or outreach) program, wonderful! If so, you will want to use this book to glean ideas to make it even better. We can always find better ways to do almost anything, can't we? You'll pick up tips and suggestions on managing your program that may not have occurred to you. You'll learn how others have tracked their progress and made mid-course corrections, when necessary. You can explore other projects that may enhance the outcome of your program. You'll find good ideas here to put to good use in your work. You'll learn the better way of doing good.

If you are contemplating starting a charitable (or philanthropic or outreach) program, this book will lead you through the process.

Maybe you see a need in your neighborhood but don't quite know how to address it. Maybe you are a part of an outreach committee that doesn't know how to maximize the impact of its annual budget. You have a vague feeling that there must be a better way to have a better outcome for your dollars.

Perhaps you have just inherited some money (or gotten a windfall profit from your business) and you would like to use that money to do something important in the world. Regardless of whether you are an individual or part of a group—starting a new program the right way will enhance your chances of success. This book will be your guide.

Finding a better way of doing good is particularly important in today's economic conditions. No one—individual, government, charitable or non-profit organization—has the same ample resources that it had previously. Cutbacks and layoffs and business failures have reduced the amount of money available for assistance programs. Individuals whose own incomes have been reduced often cut back on donations to non-profit organizations such as charities and churches. That drop in contributions reduces the funds those groups have for their work. At the same time, government revenues drop, reducing the amount of tax dollars available for aid programs. And everyone suffers. When this economic reversal happens world-wide, such as happened during the 2008 global financial crisis, the impact on the needy is multiplied. They see their own small incomes reduced at the same time as they see cutbacks in the supplemental assistance they relied on to close the subsistence gap.

But maybe, just maybe, these shrinking resources have a hidden benefit. Perhaps the decrease in available funds will prompt us to stop doing our outreach programs the same old way, spending the same amounts on the same programs that ultimately produce the same (disappointing) results. Maybe fewer funds will mean greater creativity. Maybe fewer dollars will lead to more efficiency. Maybe we will be willing to try new ideas. Maybe those shrinking resources will be the impetus to get us out of our rut.

We need to get out of business-as-usual mode of thinking and doing. In times of economic gloom, the silver lining behind all these clouds may well be that there is a new, *a better way*, of doing good. It's a better way of doing good that conserves resources, avoids costly missteps, and results in empowering people to free themselves from misery, hunger, and want.

This better way of doing good is more effective and more cost-efficient than the old way. It results in lasting change, not quick-fixes. It is effective because it attacks the causes of societal wounds rather than applying band-aids to the resulting injuries. It is cost-efficient because it solves problems once and for all instead of smoothing them over only to see them erupt again later. This better way is easy to understand, simple to implement, and satisfying for all involved.

Just follow the down-to-earth, step-by-step method presented in this book. Work your way through the A, B, C steps, taking time to digest each part before rushing on to the next chapter. This is a building process. What you learn in the first chapter will be put to use right away in the second, and so forth. When you get to the last chapter you will have assembled the framework for a better way of doing whatever good you choose to tackle.

The exercises that accompany the text are valuable as well. Don't skip them. Don't think "Oh, I'll come back to do that," or "I don't have a pen handy so I'll do this later." Do it now. Do the exercise while the text is fresh in your mind. You'll be surprised at how much you already know. You'll find out what you suspected all along—there is a better way to do good. Once you read the text and complete the exercise, you'll experience a moment of breath-taking jubilation. You'll discover that you were right. There is a better way. And the better way of doing good is a straightforward, logical, and efficient process.

You can use this book by yourself, or you can share it with a group of like-minded persons. Perhaps your local civic association, or your church outreach committee, or your women's club wants a more effective way to accomplish its outreach or philanthropic programs. You can bring this book, and its message of better ways, to them. When you point out that by following the plan outlined here you can do more good work, more effectively, with fewer resources, you'll have an eager audience.

You can study this book by yourself or with your family. Or you can organize a study group and meet regularly to discuss what you have learned. You can use this process to set up a new program, to improve an existing program, or use the information you've uncovered to disband a program that has been a waste of time and resources.

Whether you go it alone or share the experience with others, don't delay. Just get going. Turn the page, grab a pen, and begin. Set off on your own journey to a better way of doing good—then take others with you.

Approach

In this chapter we will look at the current situation in outreach programs (or philanthropy or charity—the terms are interchangeable here). We will look at the three critical components of a good program: accomplishment, action, and advocacy. We'll learn why we need to concentrate on *why*, not *who*. And we'll learn why we are not trying to "help" anyone.

The better way of doing good. Sounds like one of those TV infomercials that promises a magical tool that will fix your car, weed your garden, and clean your house, all using only one AA battery, doesn't it? A bit too good to be true. A bit pie-in-the-sky. We smile, don't we, remembering the old adage, if it looks too good to be true, it probably is.

Well, in this case, the better way to do good is not too good to be true. We want to reach out to those in need in effective ways. We want to make our philanthropy count. We want our outreach programs to make a real, measurable difference. We want to fix the wrongs of the world. But we know that our current way is not really making much of a difference.

We want a new outreach plan that is effective, long-lasting, respectful of the environment and peoples' dignity. We want a new philanthropic model that capitalizes on the best we have to offer and avoids, so far as possible, any potential pitfalls. And we want a new charitable strategy that does all of this at a lower cost in time and resources. In short, we want to be caring, but careful. We want to be both compassionate and competent. If we can come up with a program that does all this, then we will have found the better way of doing good.

A new approach to doing good would have to be different from the programs we have become accustomed to in the past. The past isn't good enough any more. If we are going to find the better way, we will have to stop thinking in the old way. We are going to have to stop jumping on any program that professes to address some problem. We have a moral obligation to do the right thing, in the right way. We must open our minds to a new way, a better way.

This better way is built on an understanding of the elements essential to lasting change. It incorporates the lessons learned from previous programs. It is based on the expertise of those with years of experience in economic and social development—on what are now called "best practices." It is practical. It is a better way.

The principal differences to this new, better way may seem to be pretty ordinary at first glance. They may not seem to be particularly momentous or earth shattering. But believe me, this shift to a better way will make a huge difference in our effectiveness. It will change how we chose our battles, construct our strategies, and carry out our campaigns. It will help us eliminate ineffective tactics. This new approach will enable us to describe clearly what we expect to achieve—and how—and enable us to engage others in the program with us. It will enable us to stay on track, make necessary corrections midstream, and know when we have reached our goal. This seemingly minor shift in focus will have enormous payoff in the end.

We need to pause here and clarify an important issue. In this book we are going to look primarily at setting up outreach *programs*—not on individual voluntary activities. We are going to assume that you are reading this book because you are thinking of starting a new program, or revamping an old one. We hope that you are also a volunteer in already existing programs. Volunteers are incredibly important—today, tomorrow, and always. You know that your volunteerism has had wonderful benefits—for those you've worked with and for, and for yourself as well.

As the former president of a large Junior League, I am a huge proponent of volunteerism. I firmly believe that volunteers have, throughout history, made life a little easier for millions of people. Our country was built through the efforts of people helping their neighbors, whether by caring for the ill, teaching coping skills and a new language to new arrivals, or through the old-fashioned barn-raising. Volunteers are the most valuable resource we have—and have had.

And volunteerism has been a hallmark of our country since its founding. The Frenchman Alexis de Tocqueville traveled around the United States in the early nineteenth century, observing how Americans lived and thought. He remarked on the amazing volunteer spirit he saw everywhere. He attributed it to the frontier spirit. These intrepid pioneers did not feel coerced or bound to serve, so they could volunteer with pluck and pride. Americans felt themselves equal to all others, so they could be generous with their time and their resources. That is, American volunteerism emerges from a foundation of ethical and political independence.

And that spirit of volunteerism still exists. It is amazing and wonderful and responsible for a staggering amount of good work that has been done throughout the world with few resources except willing hands.

   ∾ *A church in a poor section of Ketchikan, Alaska, was concerned about family breakdown, particularly among the most destitute families in the community. They were also concerned about the children's school success and the number of adults in the community who were chronically unemployed or underemployed. So volunteers from the church formed the Ketchikan Resource Center. Every Thursday night, needy families are invited to a free dinner called "Crock Pot Luck." The volunteers cook a simple, low-cost meal in crock pots and rice cookers. Families eat the meal together (that the entire family attend together and eat together is the one requirement of the program). After dinner, volunteers help the children with their homework, while the parents participate in special sessions on topics such as parenting skills, resume preparation, health topics.* ∾

These volunteers saw a problem, figured out a program to address it, and made it happen. The cost was small, but the benefits were great. In this case, as with most development programs, volunteers were a primary resource.

In fact, most of the information you'll find in this book comes from my own experience working with and observing volunteers in action. I have seen volunteers become aware of an incredibly tough, complex problem with no easy answer. These conscientious folks came up with a plan to solve the problem. They employed every resource they had at hand to implement their plan, and they reached their goal.

If you are a volunteer now, or have been one, or plan to be one, thank you. You are part of a vast army, unpaid in cash but reaping huge compensation in the lives you have enriched.

This book is designed to build on your volunteer experience. It takes into account our human motivation to be compassionate, to correct some ill we see in the world. It describes a design for philanthropic projects that actually solves the problems that are wounding people's lives. Using the method presented in this book, you will be able to construct an effective program that will have the greatest impact at the lowest cost. By using the fewest possible resources, we will not waste resources. Any that we have leftover can be devoted to solving other problems in the next program we undertake.

This new approach is indeed a better way of doing good. It focuses on three concepts key to this approach: Accomplishment, Action, and Advocacy.

Accomplish

First, we are going to concentrate on what we want to *accomplish* rather than what we want to *do*. We are going to focus on where we want to go, not on how we are going to get there. We are going to define, carefully and plainly, what we want to change. We are going to clearly describe the problem that is creating the particular ill we want to address. We're going to get below the symptoms to the cause.

Once we know what the problem is (where we want to go), we can imagine the solution (how we're going to get there). We're going to work at this until we have a concise statement that sums up what success is going to look like. We are going to describe precisely what we expect to have accomplished at the end of the program. After all, if we are going to go to the trouble of doing something, let's be very, very clear about what we want to achieve. Remember, if you don't know where you are going, any road will lead you there.

We might think of this new approach in medical terms. A patient comes to the doctor complaining of severe abdominal pain and a very high fever. The doctor would undoubtedly prescribe a painkiller and work quickly to reduce the fever. But those efforts, necessary and useful as they are, are not cures, but are only temporary measures. Prescribing them would do nothing to treat the underlying cause. Something is creating the pain and the fever, and the doctor's next step would be to ferret out the disease and cure that.

The doctor does not confuse treating the symptoms with curing the disease. Neither should we confuse relieving hunger, or homelessness, or illness with curing the diseases causing these symptoms. Therefore, we will focus our attention on our ultimate goal, our accomplishment, rather than on the intermediary steps. Like the doctor, we should not forget to relieve the pain and reduce the fever, but we should never make the mistake of thinking that if we treat those symptoms we will have cured the underlying illness.

Let's take a couple of other examples to be sure we understand this concept. Getting to the problem instead of focusing on the symptom is key to understanding this better way of doing good.

Homelessness and hunger are both horrible circumstances, but neither is a problem to be solved. Homelessness and hunger are not problems—they are manifestations of problems. They are evidence of a deeper, more systemic problem.

People may be homeless for a number of different reasons. Their homes may have been destroyed in a natural disaster such as a hurricane, or in a civil disaster such as war. They may be homeless because they are unemployed and cannot pay rent. A mother and her children may have escaped an abusive spouse with only their clothes and a few dollars.

Temporary shelters for these people certainly treat the symptom, just as painkiller and fever reducers treat the symptoms of a threatening disease. And we must pay attention and relieve the symptoms. But we cannot confuse treating the symptoms with solving the problem. Useful as they are, the shelters don't solve the problem that created the homelessness in the first place.

Likewise, people may be hungry for a variety of causes. Is there simply not enough food to be had? Are the grocery shelves well stocked, but the hungry don't have enough money to buy food? Are they refugees fleeing a savage rebellion? Are they too sick with malaria to farm their small acreage?

Food handouts will provide short-term relief but will not, in the long-run, solve the problem of hunger. For that we need to figure out what created the crisis and focus our attention on fixing that.

So our first step in this new approach to a better way of doing good is to focus on what problem we want to solve, and what the solution would look like if we accomplished it. Now turn to Exercise 1-1 (Causes, not Symptoms) to see if you can identify the root causes, rather than the symptoms, of some major humanitarian concerns.

Causes, not Symptoms

See if you can think of at least four causes for each of the conditions below.

We've repeated the causes of hunger from Chapter 1 to get you started.

HUNGER   Drought
                No money
                Too sick to work
                Refugees from civil war

HOMELESSNESS

ILL-HEALTH

ILLITERACY

What have you discovered about the difference between the symptom (hunger, for example) and the cause?

_____

_____

_____

Can you give one example of a "better way" to prevent people from being hungry rather than just giving them some food?

_____

_____

_____

Action

Next, we are going to focus on the activities that would solve the problem, not on the people who are affected by the problem. We are going to talk about *why* and *what*, not about *who*. We are not going to focus on the people who are homeless or hungry or sick. They are not the problem. Their unfortunate condition is a result of the problem. We must focus our attention and our actions on the problem, not on those who suffer as a result of the problem.

Don't mistake me here. I am as softhearted as anyone about those who are suffering. I too would feed every hungry person, and house every homeless child—but I know those actions alone won't solve the *problem*. Because the problem isn't *them* (nor is it hunger or homelessness—the symptoms), the problem is whatever is creating the hunger and homelessness in the first place. We need to concentrate on solving the *why*. When we do, we will know what to do, and *who* will then reap the benefits. Now turn to Exercise 1-2 on page 10 to practice seeing the difference between Symptoms and Actions.

To be certain that we keep our attention focused on the right target, we should never describe our objective or our actions in terms of people. The people are not the problem. They are the survivors of the problem. They are weighted down by the problem. They can't break its hold. To focus our attention on people diverts us from seeing clearly the origin of their misery and knowing how to fix it.

To prevent our slipping into the old mode, we are going to outlaw one word as we go forward. Danger lurks when we focus on *helping* instead of *solving*. Too often when we think in terms of helping people (an activity), we think of doing *to* them, or *for* them. Neither one is the right approach. Neither one is appropriate. People are not objects. We don't do something *to* them. And doing *for* them is treating them as children or as incapable.

Symptoms versus Actions

See if you can think of at least four actions you might take to solve the problem of two of the causes of hunger.

HUNGER   Drought

Too sick to work

What have you discovered about the difference between the symptom (hunger, for example) and the actions needed to solve the problem?

_____

_____

_____

_____

Oh, sure, sometimes helping is the right thing to do (the Boy Scout oath, for sure, requires the boys to be "helpful"). We help the old lady across the street. We help our children with their homework. We help out at the local street fair.

These kinds of helpfulness—these activities—are wonderful and important and to be encouraged. They result in crossing the street, in homework done, a successful street fair. But they are different from the kind of "helping" that we're talking about here. These kinds of activities treat symptoms.

The helping that we decry is the helping that is an activity that masquerades as a solution to a problem. If we avoid using the term *help*, we will avoid falling into the trap of thinking that we have actually changed the system instead of merely smoothing over the symptom. If we avoid the word *help*, we will avoid focusing on people rather than problems.

In *A River Runs Through It, and Other Stories* by Norman Maclean, the father is speaking:

> ∞ *So it is . . . that we can seldom help anybody. Either we don't know what part to give or maybe we don't like to give any part of ourselves. Then more often than not, the part that is needed is not wanted. And even more often, we do not have the part that is needed.* ∞

So in this book, we will never use the word *help* to describe our work to do good a better way. We're talking about something more important, more vital that merely "helping." We're talking about a better way to make lasting change in the world.

You have undoubtedly been involved in assistance programs in the past. You've reached out to someone in need. You've been part of a philanthropic or charitable group. You've acted on your charitable impulses. Thank you.

Or maybe you are considering starting a program, or are right in the middle of one. You want to do some good, but you suspect that there are better ways than you've used in the past. Great! Recognizing the need for a better way can always result in improvements. We can move forward only when we recognize that the old way may not be the best way anymore. It may have been the best way at one time or at least the best way that we knew of at that time. But times have changed, and we have learned a lot. It is silly to keep on doing good in the same old way when better ways now exist. Remember the old definition of a fool? Someone who continues to do the same thing in the same way, expecting a different result. You and I aren't fools—we don't want to continue the same kind of work in the same way if we aren't getting the best results. And now there is a simple process to a different way to get better results.

Don't get me wrong. Even our old ways have certainly had a positive impact on people's lives. We've been doing the very best that we can. We've been learning as we go, trying to put into practice those things that work. And we have had some successes. But if you are like me (and I suspect that you are or you wouldn't be anxious to find better ways to change the world), you've been a bit dissatisfied with the results. We just haven't made as big an impact as we had hoped for.

But we have learned from our successes and from our mistakes. And we have learned from others who have the same altruistic impulses that we have. If we consolidate all our findings, we can develop a new strategy that promises to bring about true, lasting change. That's what this book is all about. This book is about the better way.

Advocacy

Finally, we will disabuse ourselves of the notion that we must always tackle a problem directly. Head-on doesn't always work. Sometimes we have to address barriers that would prevent the obvious solution. Therefore, we often need to change attitudes, or cultural mores, or laws.

Parents who have been raised in a culture that doesn't value education for girls aren't suddenly going to welcome a new all-girls' school building. A society that hides children with birth defects isn't going to support vocational training programs for the disabled. A country in the throes of civil war between ethnic groups is not going to set up refugee camps for "enemies" from the other side. Some problems are simply not fixable within the existing structure. Sometimes the best way to accomplish lasting change is to change the system, the culture that creates the problem in the first place.

The late Kenneth Bacon, a friend of mine, was president of Refugees International, an organization that is a worldwide advocate for those displaced by war or natural disasters. He was quoted in the *Wall Street Journal* on August 17, 2009, as pointing out that when we focus on fixing the system, we can "not only take care of the refugees, [we] can end the problem that created the refugees in the first place." Housing and feeding refugees are important and humanitarian goals. But the better way of doing good is to stop the conditions that cause people to flee their homes.

Advocacy can mean working to change the system or the culture. It can mean changing restrictive laws. It can also mean speaking on behalf of those who cannot speak for themselves. Those silent ones need advocates who can represent their needs, their frustrations, and their obstacles to those in a position to effect the necessary corrections. Frequently, such advocacy results in better outcomes than direct action would be.

One need not be a high-powered lobbyist or a well-connected citizen to create such change. Think of the enormous culture shift that has occurred because of the work of Mothers Against Drunk Driving. The founders could not stop each potentially dangerous inebriated driver. What they could do was stop our tolerance for such actions and encourage more stringent sentencing.

These three components of our new approach (Accomplishment, Action, Advocacy) will be the basis of our better way of doing good. You will find this new, systematic approach easy to understand and implement. It will save you time and trouble. This approach will remove some of the bigger rocks on which we might stub our well-meaning toes. This approach will let you or your group start out with a clear sense of mission. You'll know what you want to achieve. You'll have confidence in your actions. You'll be able to measure your effectiveness. You'll know how and when to make mid-course corrections. And best of all, you'll make a real difference in the lives of those in need.

Isn't that the better way to do good?

Summary

As we go forward, then, we will remember that much has already been accomplished to aid those in need around the world. Much progress has been made in education, health, human services, nutrition, and housing. But much more needs yet to be done. We recognize that reduced resources at all levels will mean that we need to work smarter in order to achieve further gains. We are convinced that there is a better way to do good.

We have identified three areas in our prior approach to doing good that need to be changed. These three changes will crop up again and again in the following chapters. We know now that we must focus on what we want to Accomplish, determine the appropriate Action to take, and the importance of including Advocacy among our options.

Basics

How many times have you heard it said—back to basics? You have to learn the basics. Whether you are learning to cook (what does braise mean anyhow?) or play tennis ("love–15"?), or speak a foreign language (*voulez-vous* what?), you have to learn the fundamentals. The same is true in good works.

The better way to do good starts with several basic pieces of the puzzle. Put them all together, and one creates a meaningful picture. Using the exercises that accompany this chapter will give you all the tools you need to investigate your program Choices.

Unfortunately, we seem to believe that we are born with the ability to solve other people's problems with just our own goodwill.

We embark on good deeds believing that we will make a difference if we rely solely on our good intentions. When we start a program of assistance, or a project to correct some ill in the world, do we even consider that our program might fail? Of course not. When we dedicate time, energy, and resources into making the world a better place, we expect that our efforts will achieve our goals. When we run into obstacles, or when events don't unfold as we expected, we get frustrated. Where did we go wrong? we ask.

Our good intentions weren't to blame. Probably we just didn't take the time to learn the basics of good programming. Maybe we thought that our good intentions were enough, even though we knew that others before us had tried to fix the problem with equally good intentions and that the problem hadn't gone away, it was still with us.

Certainly we need to have good intentions before we start. We must be convinced that we can solve the problem, that we can make a difference in the world. We must believe that we can do it. You already know that.

You also recognize that if we don't believe our endeavor will be fruitful, it probably won't be. There's an old saying "If you believe you can't, you are probably right." Why? Well, we won't give our full attention and our full wisdom to the undertaking. Our skepticism will undermine our efforts. We won't be able to engage others in the program as they will readily sense our doubts.

A few folks start projects with only half-hearted enthusiasm. Sometimes they have been cajoled into participating. Sometimes they know what the problem is but don't trust that they can solve it. They want to do good; they suspect that a better way exists; but they just don't where to find it.

While such uncertainty is never a good start, we can learn a useful lesson from those who question their capacity to solve problems. Their hesitation serves as a valuable reminder of the need to be sure we know what we are undertaking. We need to avoid either jumping in with both feet, gung-ho, or reluctantly dragging ourselves to do something when we doubt we can finish it. We should, instead, step back and appraise the situation with a more skeptical eye.

If the solution to such problems was so apparent that one could jump right in, the problems would no longer exist. If such problems were easily cleared up, someone would have done so already. With no shortage of well-meaning people in the world, we would have no problems left if all problems were easily solved.

And many of the easy ones have been solved. We can rejoice in that. Their solution means that people around the world have benefitted from good works. Great strides have been made in making people's lives easier because some of their problems have been tackled and conquered. The easy problems have been taken care of. Still, problems remain. And the ones that do remain are the ones that are trickiest to solve.

So we cannot avoid the hard problems. We have to turn our attention to the more difficult, the more intractable ones. As President Obama said on April 2, 2009, at the meeting of the G-20 in London: "We've solved the simple problems. The problems that remain are the obdurate, tricky, complex ones."

The kinds of evils that remain are not susceptible to quick fixes. They are still bedeviling us precisely because they are difficult to deal with.

That doesn't mean that we should throw up our hands and walk away. Someone has to tackle these problems, and we're as capable as anyone. We just need to go about it in the right way. And barreling ahead with little forethought and planning is not the right way. There is, however, a simple and a better way.

In order to *accomplish* (remember Chapter 1?), we must start with the problem rather than with what actions we might take. We must determine the nature of the problem and imagine what a solution might look like. To do that, we can take advantage of good information out there. We can do our homework and learn about the recognized "best practices" of philanthropy. Once we have begun to sketch out our philanthropic map, we can learn how to choose a route to the solution. In short, we need to start at the beginning. We need to start with the basics to the better way of doing good.

Just as we must master the basics before we become proficient in any new skill, we must master the basics of outreach, of philanthropy, before we can make the best use of our resources and our initiative. We don't expect to play at Wimbledon before we learn the basics of serve and volley. We don't expect to be hired as a master chef before we learn the basics of braise and poach. We don't expect to write love letters before we learn penmanship and spelling (or, in today's world, before we learn to type and use spell-check).

Just so, we need to take a little time to learn the basics of doing good the better way before we start. Effective philanthropy is built on time-tested principles. Efficient outreach programs depend on the best practices developed by experienced, exemplary non-profit organizations. We can build on their key concepts in order to organize our own thoughts as we go forward.

Philanthropy, or outreach, also has a specific vocabulary. By learning "development speak," we recognize the special meaning of words such as *partnership*, *evaluation*, and *sustainability* in the philanthropic context. Terms such as *community participation* and *memorandum of understanding* are important concepts in developing and managing outreach programs. By coming to a common understanding of terms generally used in the outreach arena, we will reduce the chance of misunderstanding. Especially for groups—whether outreach committees, or civic or social organizations which want to engage in philanthropic activities—learning to speak the development language will be invaluable in allowing all members to communicate as the group sets priorities, determines roles, and measures success.

First of all, we need to distinguish clearly between three key development terms: *resource, activity*, and *result*. These concepts are so important that we need to spend a bit more time to be sure we all understand the nuances of each. In "development speak" the three concepts of resource, activity, and result are often called *input, output,* and *impact*. We will use the terms interchangeably so you will get used to working in either vocabulary.

Resources (or Inputs)

Resource refers to the assets *put into* the project. Those inputs may be tangible, such as money, equipment, building space, or tools. Intangible inputs are equally important: talent, passion, enthusiasm, creativity, expertise. All projects rely on adequate resources. Most successful projects need several separate kinds of resources. Generally, projects use different inputs at different times in the life of the project. For example, starting a new project will require a great deal of passion and creativity; later the program will require more tangible resources and will often need new inputs of expertise of different kinds.

Because most folks are unaware of the panoply of resources (inputs) available to them, let's spend a bit more time being sure we search out all those that might help us. We have far more resources, and kinds of resources, available to us than we would believe at first. When we deliberately sit down and catalogue our resources, we come up with an amazing amount.

What exactly do we mean by "resources"? A resource is any asset, or attribute, or quality, or supply that can be gathered and channeled so it can be employed in a philanthropic program. Most commonly, when we think of resources, we think of money. And money is an important resource. But it is not the only one. Other resources can include:

- Talent
- Abilities
- Expertise
- Experience
- Skill
- Contacts
- Knowledge
- Vision
- Creativity
- Imagination
- Things (books, tools, cars)
- Buildings and other real estate

And don't forget *passion*, which is an incredible resource.

Let's take a moment to look at some of these categories and see what unrecognized resources you might have available.

Please beware here: At this point, we are not asking whether the talent or the expertise, or whatever, is useful for the outreach program or programs you are considering. We are simply trying to catalogue all the many resources that you can think of that would be on hand or that you could obtain if you should decide you need them. Once you decide upon a program and the activities you might undertake, then you can narrow down your list to the applicable resources. Conversely, on occasion, knowing what inputs you could draw upon may well guide you in the selection of your program and the activities that you will undertake. A program that you might dearly like to tackle may require resources that you have no way to obtain. Whether to start with your resources first or your program first is a bit of a two-way street, but since we must start somewhere, let's concentrate here on resources. Let's not let the horse (the program) get before the cart (the catalogue of available inputs).

Talent

Can you, or someone in your group, organize, manage, persuade, tell stories, sing, paint, draw, write? Is someone the most creative brainstormer you know (in other words, comes up with the wackiest ideas)? Do you have someone who has the ability to facilitate a discussion so that all participants feel their views have been heard? As you are thinking about these categories, assume that a talent or ability is something innate in the person, as opposed to a skill that one might have been taught. Here we are looking for *aptitudes* more than *occupations* or trades.

Start a list of those people with talents and abilities. You can't imagine at this point how a talent might be used, so at this point your goal is to think of as many different talents as possible.

Here's an example of how one talent could be used:

> ✤ *A young man in a small community plays the piano by ear. He has never had a lesson in his life. Even though he is employed full time, he makes time to go to the senior center every Tuesday evening at dinner hour and plays in the dining room. The seniors love to hear the old tunes; they sing along and tap their canes to the beat. In a way he is solving their problems of loneliness and lack of stimulation.* ✤

Solving problems can require a whole set of talents and abilities. Can you, or can you find, someone who can sing? Negotiate and soothe ruffled feathers? Very often we discover that our friends and acquaintances have abilities we never guessed. A good friend of mine was head of fundraising for a major health organization. Diann and I also worked together in the same social service volunteer organization. I knew her for some time before I found out that she had once taught in high school in Australia and that she was in great demand all around the country as a judge at ice-skating competitions. I could envision several ways we could use her talent for teaching. (I'm still trying to figure out how we can capitalize on her knowledge of ice-skating techniques.)

Other individuals have abilities that they may have not had occasion to use in years. Think of Grandpa Ralph's skill in fixing an antique auto's carburetor or Aunt Ruth's ability to make each member of the family feel like the most special person in her life.

Survey your group, or your circle of friends, or the members of your congregation or civic association. Make a game of it. See if you can document ten, or twenty, or forty different talents that would be available—should you need them. At this point, we are just collecting information, not assessing its usefulness. Who knows, Grandma Hattie's fantastic memory may be useful when we need to know the kinds of childhood games she and her friends played eighty years ago when we undertake a project at the local historical museum!

So ferret out the obvious, the less apparent, and the hidden talents of your group.

Now turn to Exercise 2-1. The questions there are designed to trigger your thinking about talents and abilities that may be available to you. Do this exercise before continuing with the next section. This is a step-by-step process, and you don't want to stumble because you missed a step along the way.

Professional or Avocational Expertise

Are you a business person, a doctor, a landscaper, a tennis coach, a farmer. Are you a world traveler? Do you know a social worker, an entrepreneur, a golf pro?

> *A South African woman named Allison knew how to make quilts. She also knew that single mothers living in a shantytown on the outskirts of Cape Town, South Africa, were illiterate and had no way to buy food for their children or pay public school fees (which are standard in South Africa). She knew that the women often hand-embroidered native Xhosa designs on their skirts and blouses. So she volunteered to teach the women how to use that skill to make quilts. A local community service organization donated space. Allison found an American group to donate money to purchase sewing machines, cloth, and thread.*

Talents and Abilities

We're going to stretch our minds to find unusual talents or abilities among our family and acquaintances. (Remember, our definition of talent or ability is something that we were born with, not something that we acquired by experience or education.)

Two examples:

> My neighbor has a talent for seeing beauty amid the most mundane flowers along the side of the road, and creating gorgeous arrangements out of them.

> My son has an amazing ability to train dogs—he just seems to know what they are thinking and how to get them to behave.

Now, think of one significant talent or ability for each of the following:

- A family member or one of your in-laws

- Your next-door or across-the-street neighbor (either side)

- Your best high-school buddy

- Your minister, pastor, rabbi, or other spiritual director

- The waiter at your favorite restaurant

- Your closest friend

- Your least-favorite acquaintance

- The chair of your book/woman's/social/civic club

- Your golfing/tennis/bridge/chess partner

- Your spouse or significant other

The women embroidered the Xhosa designs on the quilt blocks by hand, then learned to use sewing machines (a new skill) to stitch the blocks together. The women also had to learn to measure accurately, calculate needed supplies, and meet work deadlines (more new skills). They brought two enormous advantages to the partnership: they were creative, and they were highly motivated—inputs that they could provide to the project.

When the women had finished several expert-quality quilts, Allison persuaded a local tourist shop to stock them. A buyer for Liberty's of London department store saw the quilts and ordered six dozen for the London store. And then a developer, who was building a hotel in Cape Town, ordered a quilt for each of the hotel bedrooms.

Now the women had an occupation. They had an income. They had dignity. And all because of Allison, who knew how to quilt. ✎

Think of the different professions practiced in your community. Think of people you know who have an interesting hobby. A retired stamp collector in Virginia has just written a book illustrating the history of Williamsburg through stamps. This unusual approach could excite a ho-hum student who previously saw history as boring and irrelevant.

Now turn to Exercise 2-2 and document the expertise or skills or vocations or hobbies of twelve or more people who might be useful to your outreach effort.

Contacts

Whom do you know who has contacts that could be useful? Someone with political contacts? Someone who knows a good fundraiser, or non-profit accountant, or journalist? A student who can put you in touch with a professor at the local college in the field you are investigating?

Particularly if you are considering a program in a foreign location, you are wise to find persons familiar with the culture, mores, legal systems,

Persons with Expertise

We're going to make a list of at least twelve people we know who might be willing to share their professional or avocational expertise with us. The obvious ones are lawyers, doctors, and teachers. But think a little more out of the box. See how many people you know who have unusual expertise.

Then guess, on a scale of 1–5, whether that person would likely assist you in an outreach program (1 being probably, 5 being probably not). Don't ask them now. This isn't the time. Just use your best judgment.

Name	Expertise	Likely/Unlikely

politics, religions, and economy of that area. International development agencies never try to launch a program in a new area without finding a local partner to guide them through the intricacies of the local environment. In addition, they confer with other agencies that operate programs in the region, in order to avoid wasteful duplication. By collaborating they often fill critical gaps in development services.

If you can find someone in your community who grew up or has worked in that country, you should make every effort to engage him or her in your program. Such people have key knowledge of the customs, resources, and services already present and may well have contacts in-country that will prove extremely useful. They can be a key go-between if you decide to partner with a local person or group. They can be an enormous help to both partners, moving the program along and smoothing possible misunderstandings. Contacts in for-profit organizations can prove extremely helpful.

> ∽ *A small civic group was concerned that high school graduates in the public schools in a neighboring low-income town were unable to get entry level jobs because they lacked computer skills. They discovered that the public schools could not afford enough computers to teach every student, although they had the space and a willing teacher.*
>
> *One member of the civic group knew a highly placed executive in a large corporation nearby (the contact!). With some negotiation between the group, the school administration, and the corporation, the corporation agreed to donate their old computers to the school each time it purchased new upgraded ones. Over time, this program resulted in the school having an exemplary computer-training program. High school students learned sufficient computer skills to enable them to get good jobs in the area, even jobs with the donating corporation.* ∽

 Particularly if you are considering an advocacy program, the more highly placed people you know (or know how to contact), the greater chance you will have to succeed. Successful advocacy requires influence. Influence can result from the combined power of many individual voices (as in a mass movement such as MADD) or from the attention generated by a few widely recognized voices. The "Make Poverty History" campaign owes a great deal of its success to the highly visible involvement of Bono and U2. *Someone knew how to contact them.*

Look over the list of persons you named in Exercises 2-1 and 2-2. Do any of them have highly placed or influential contacts that you might call upon?

The Big Three

Now we come to the three resources that are probably more important than all the others combined when it comes to solving problems: vision, creativity, and imagination.

Vision

Without a vision of the future, without the ability to conjure up a picture of the world as we want it to be, we risk running aimlessly down dead-end paths. Vision alone, of course, won't get us to the result we want. The Japanese have a proverb that captures the relationship between vision and action:

> *Vision without action is a daydream.*
> *Action without vision is a nightmare.*

Creativity

People have been trying to solve the problems of the world for centuries. The old ways just haven't worked. What we need is new creativity. We need creative people to devise fresh methods of tackling seemingly intractable problems. We need creative people to develop new ways to farm, to mine, to fish, to teach. We need creativity—the more the better.

Imagination

Along with creativity, we need people with imagination. We want people who can imagine an entirely different future. People who can imagine new ways for people to interact. People who can invent and concoct. The great Canadian humorist, Stephen B. Leacock, once said, "It may be those who do most, dream most." Let's dream about what might be done and then do it.

We want to dream big dreams. Remember Martin Luther King's "I Have a Dream" speech? That dream changed history. That vision of a better America changed how we thought and how we acted. That vision led us to a more just world.

Who do you know that is amazingly creative? Who is the most imaginative person in your group? Who is always coming up with the wildest, out-of-the-box idea that just might work? Get them on your team and come up with spectacular new ways to make a difference. Of course not all of them will work. Some will be downright ridiculous. But at least consider the far-out ones. While you have to tread carefully—the line between creativity and lunacy is sometimes unclear—you are looking for bright new ideas. That's the better way.

Tangible Resources

Finally, we are going to think about the kind of resources that come most readily to people's minds. Supplies and goods and food and bricks and mortar and things. But even though these are the most commonly mentioned resources, we rarely exhaust our scope of just what might be included in this category. Many, many more inputs are available to us than we would ordinarily consider. So let's look at some examples.

Things What things do you have, or have access to, that could be useful? These items need not be new, but they do need to be appropriate.

> ∽ *According to recent reports, thrift stores are suddenly thriving, as people realize that they can find serviceable clothes, shoes, and household goods for a fraction of the price of new goods. This is a win-win-win situation. Those on limited incomes can purchase goods for a fraction of the cost at the traditional department stores; the non-profit running the thrift shop, such as a hospital auxiliary, raises funds for its cause; the donors get a nice tax-deduction for their unneeded goods.*

> *Habitat for Humanity has started a new program to re-sell materials removed during home renovations. In particular, kitchen cabinets and appliances are recycled; the homeowner receives a tax-deduction, and the purchaser gets gently used items at a discount. Habitat for Humanity uses the sale proceeds to support its home-building programs around the world.*

Items no longer of use in one location might be priceless in another. A woman in Connecticut had a vacation home on an island in the Caribbean. She was appalled to learn that the school libraries were almost empty; they had few books of any sort. School administrators complained that their budgets were so small that they could not afford to buy books, much as they would like to. They also complained that the only book store on the island sold primarily adult novels geared to the tourist trade, so they could not purchase appropriate books locally.

The Connecticut woman contacted the Kiwanis Club in her town and told them that if they would collect and box books, she would pay to ship the books and would also pay any necessary customs duties. In just a few months, hundreds of boxes of books were on their way to the schools in Turks and Caicos.

But our generous woman didn't stop there. Turks and Caicos is a golfers' paradise for tourists. The local children are often given used golf equipment by generous tourists, but they rarely play because they can't afford to buy golf balls. As part of her strategy to give the children on the island more opportunities, she attended a golf tournament in Connecticut and asked the players to donate all their leftover balls. She collected baskets full of balls to take with her on her next trip to Turks and Caicos. ✿

What "things" can you come up with that would be useful to someone in need?

Before you start making a list, consider the following warnings.

Always consider the possible impact that your providing "things" may have on the local community. Taking, or sending, goods to an impoverished area can have devastating effects on the local economy. Goods that are given away deprive the local merchant of a sale. Those shopkeepers need each small sale in order to support their families. With the sales proceeds they buy food or clothing from other local merchants, who then support their families, and so on. Each dollar spent is estimated to circulate seven times.

Therefore, bringing or sending goods into such an area can be damaging if the goods are available for purchase there. If you are thinking of shipping or taking supplies to a needy area, be sure that the supplies aren't available for purchase there. School children in Nairobi may not have pens and pencils, but the local general store sells them. If you send pens and pencils from here, or take them with you on a visit, you deprive the local business of a sale. Then the shopkeeper has a harder time buying food for his family; hence the grocer is deprived of a sale . . . and the cycle goes on.

Here's an example from just a few years ago:

> ∾ *A well-meaning church group visited a church-sponsored housing project in Honduras and was told the hired workmen needed shovels. The group returned to the States, canvassed their neighbors for spare used shovels, and prepared to ship them to Honduras. Fortunately, at the last moment, they learned that a hardware store only two miles from the housing project sold shovels. Instead of spending money on shipping old tools, the group sent the money to Honduras so the workmen could buy shovels. The workmen got their needed shovels (new ones at that), and the local purchase supported the community's economy.* ∾

Be especially careful of shipping goods to foreign lands. Three dangers lurk: First, the cost of shipping the goods may be exorbitant—far more than the goods are worth. Therefore, finding a source of the goods closer to the intended destination might be a better way. Second, consider customs duties, which can be onerous. Also, someone on the receiving end has to go to the port to claim the goods and pay the duties. That may not be an easy task. Third, remember that the mail delivery system in most lesser-developed areas is rarely reliable and secure. Almost every person involved in foreign development programs tells tales of "disappearing" materials and goods. For all these reasons, most development programs strive to purchase locally as much as they possibly can.

In cases of natural or civil disasters, "things" are often gathered for people whose lives and homes have been devastated. Hurricanes, tsunamis, ice storms, and war can leave people destitute. But before sending things, first be sure that needed items cannot be purchased locally. The 2004 tsunami ravaged the coast of Sri Lanka, but the flooding continued inland for only a very short distance, a matter of a few miles. Beyond the narrow coastal band of destruction, daily life was totally unaffected. Shops were open and fully stocked with all daily necessities.

Certainly those devastated by the tsunami needed food and water, but to have shipped these items to Sri Lanka would have been extremely foolish. Food and drink were not their problem—they could easily obtain those from local stores. The survivors needed quite different outreach: housing, replacement of lost fishing boats, counseling for grief. The unaffected local shop owners needed the business, since many of those in their usual customer base had been killed or displaced.

Secondly, be sure that the goods are useful and appropriate.

> *Example 1: After the earthquakes in El Salvador in 2001, one aid group sent arctic-weight sleeping bags and high-heeled shoes—totally useless items in a tropical and very rocky country.*

> *Example 2: When the Kosovo refugees were living in tents in Albania in the winter of 1999, with rain every day and mud everywhere, a group of American students gathered and sent stuffed toys for the displaced children—a well-meaning gesture, certainly, but those children really needed rubber boots, not toys that would soon be wet and dirty.*

Buildings Often overlooked as resources are buildings. Churches or civic centers or school buildings frequently sit empty a large part of the time. Could they be made available for others to use?

> *A small theater group rehearsed and performed in the rented basement of a retail business. Because most of the actors held daytime jobs, all the theater activities took place in the evening. Like most small non-profit performing groups, they were perpetually strapped for cash. Fundraising was slow; the small size of their performance space limited their ticket revenues. They cast about looking for other sources of funds.*

> *With the approval of their landlord, they sublet their space on Sunday mornings to a newly formed church group; they sublet the space Monday through Friday afternoons to an after-school tutoring program, and they sublet one room on Saturday morning to a senior-citizens' Pilates exercise class. Of course, they checked their insurance policy to be sure they had proper coverage, and signed written contracts with each sub-lessee. This creative use of space*

left them enough time for their rehearsals and performances and earned additional funds to operate their theater in the black. ∽

To what other philanthropic uses could buildings be put? Or parking lots? Or undeveloped land?

> ∽ *A passionate gardener named Marta was concerned that residents of public housing apartments in a small northeastern town had inadequate diets because they could not afford fresh vegetables. She talked with mothers in the community and learned that they would like to grow their own vegetables. Unfortunately, because they lived in apartments, they had no land for garden plots.*
>
> *Marta knew of a vacant lot owned by the town. She assembled a coalition of concerned, influential citizens to convince the town to turn the vacant lot into a community garden. She developed plans to canvas local businesses to donate the needed supplies: fencing, hoses, shovels, hoes, compost, seeds, and fertilizer. She involved the local garden club and the Master Gardeners to provide training for the new gardeners.* ∽

Think of the resources that went into this project: A visionary person, with the contacts to persuade fellow citizens to advocate with the town government; a vacant lot; a team of solicitors who promised to approach businesses for donations of necessary supplies; a garden club to provide expertise—all this to provide better nutrition.

Note that this was not a project to "help" people. This was a project to solve a problem—poor nutrition.

I hope that by now you've noticed that not once have we mentioned the resource that generally comes first to people's minds: *money*. Money is important, no doubt. Money can supplement or replace or purchase many of the other resources. Instead of finding a volunteer, you can hire an expert. Instead of collecting donated merchandise, you can purchase it. Instead of providing a community garden, you can purchase and distribute fresh vegetables.

Using money to purchase supplies or expertise is often expedient. It can solve a dire situation quickly. And sometimes time is of the essence.

Getting medicine to injured people, getting food and water to persons in a disaster area, paying the back rent to prevent the closing of a food bank—all these problems can be solved quickly by cash.

What is sacrificed, however, is the sense of community and self-reliance that is developed by collective action. The greater the number of people who are involved in solving a problem, the greater likelihood that the solution will be a good one, the right one. And the greater likelihood that the solution will be sustainable.

Remember the old adage: Give a man a fish, you feed him for today; teach him to fish, and you feed him for the rest of his life. Certainly if we give someone a fish, or money to buy a fish, he will eat today, but he will be hungry again tomorrow. If we shelter a homeless person tonight, he or she will still be homeless tomorrow. In these cases, money will solve the immediate crisis, but does nothing to solve the underlying problem: hunger or homelessness.

Teaching someone to fish is better, so long as the fish population holds up, the water doesn't get polluted, and the fishing boat doesn't develop leaks. Furthermore, teaching one person to fish may feed one hungry person, or one hungry family, but does nothing for the hungry community.

Far better to teach the community to build and manage fish ponds. They then have control over the production of protein for their diet. They learn a skill that may enable them to raise surplus fish to sell in the local market, contributing to their collective well-being. The small farmer will buy the fish; the fisherman will buy the farmer's tomatoes and peppers. Both benefit, and both have a greater variety of nutritious food.

So money may temporarily relieve the suffering, but it is not the only way, nor even the best way, to solve the problem. Certainly money can be important, and having money to spend can make or break a project, but we should never be held back because we don't have money or think we don't have enough. As we have done in this chapter, we need to look at all sorts of other resources before we even begin to talk about money.

Relying on money has a more insidious effect—that of the "Lady Bountiful" syndrome. This phrase refers to an old-fashioned idea of charity, where the well-to-do (usually pictured as an amply endowed, fashionably dressed dowager) indulges her sense of *noblesse oblige* by distributing cash to the less well-off. She gives out of a sense of duty. The grateful beneficiaries are "kept in their place," obsequious and fawning.

Over the centuries, novels and operas have been based on tales of resentment stirred up by Lady Bountiful actions; indeed, revolutions have been started over such callous displays of charity.

Even though we no longer believe that Marie Antoinette actually said, "Let them eat cake," that myth exemplifies the Lady Bountiful attitude. We must be careful that we do not fall into the trap of believing that giving poor people some money will solve their problems. Indeed, sometimes it exacerbates the problems.

> ∽ *A group of tourists were traveling by bus through a dusty, very poor village in Mexico. They had been warned not to give money to children begging at the side of the road. One white-haired older woman ignored the warning and thrust her arm out of the bus window to give a twenty-dollar bill to a particularly darling little girl. As the bus pulled away several larger boys jumped from behind the fence, knocked the little girl down in the dust, snatched the bill, and took off. The little girl sat there crying until one boy came back, grabbed her roughly, slapped her, and told her to "get back to work." ∽*

Cash is important, at the right place and at the right time, but it isn't a panacea. It is only one, and not even the most important, of the resources that we might draw upon to solve problems. From the many and varied inputs that we might be able to tap into, we have to choose the most appropriate one or ones to dedicate to our project. These resources are the fuel for the activities (the outputs) of the project.

Strange as it may sound, knowing what resources/inputs you can draw on will sometimes even determine just which problem you decide to address. An inventory of your resources is a useful guide to selecting the size, location, type, scope, time frame, and even the goal of your efforts. Put another way, your analysis of the available resources will give you a solid tool to use in selecting the right *what* you want to accomplish.

Now we look at putting those resources, those inputs, to work. This is where we start looking at the *how*, *when*, *where*, and with *whom*.

[handwritten: Activities = Outputs Process]

Activities (or Outputs)

[handwritten: Create change Activity is the strategy]

Activities (or *outputs*) and results (or *impact*) are more difficult concepts than resources (*inputs*), harder to understand right off the bat, and often confused. Activities/outputs create change; results/impacts are the changes themselves.

Activities (*outputs*) are intermediary steps that use the resources (*inputs*) to lead us to the solution, the desired result (the *impact*). Think of the activity as the process, and the impact as the goal. The following two illustrations will differentiate between the concepts.

> ∞ *Let's go back to that community garden. Remember that the problem was poor nutrition among the apartment dwellers. We saw resources of creativity, persuasion, vacant lots, donations of seeds and tools. The activity was the creation of the community garden, with its many garden plots ready for tilling and sowing, and expert guidance available, leading to the subsequent harvest of vegetables. The result, the impact, was better nutrition.*
>
> *Or think of the theater group. Their problem was viability. Their resource was their unused space. The activities were getting their landlord's permission, finding suitable subtenants, and subletting their space. The result was financial stability. Recognize too the benefit to the sub-lessees. They needed space for their activities so they could achieve their goals. They were both partners and beneficiaries in this multi-benefit program.* ∞

[handwritten: Results = Impact Changes themselves Solution]

Results (or Impact)

Not recognizing the difference between activities and results will often result in lots of wasted effort, wheel-spinning, and frustration. The common mistake is to focus on the activity rather than the hoped-for result. In short, in this case, the process is not the point!

Assume that you are concerned that children in a local school are not getting a well-rounded education. After considerable research and discussion with teachers and administrators, you decide that one major factor is that the school library does not contain the so-called "classic" books: Shakespeare, Goethe, Cervantes, etc. So you mount a campaign to raise money to purchase those books.

The resources here are passion, diligence, expertise in fundraising, and ultimately funds for purchases.

The activities are the purchase of books.

The expected result is a student body that is more well-read and, therefore, receiving a more rounded education.

Put another way, the activity is the strategy; the result is the solution to the problem—the impact. Both resources and activities can generally be counted or measured. We know how many books our project purchased. We know what kind of books we purchased. One could even make a case that the dollars raised by the fundraising campaign were activities, since they resulted from the creativity and effort of those engaged in the project; they were not inherent resources that we had when we began. All of these are "outputs"—the result of the resources. But none of them are "results." They are only intermediate steps in our activity.

Results, or impacts, are frequently far more difficult to count, to measure. That does not make them less important; indeed, if we can clearly identify the desired solution we are likely to have the key to designing a successful project. In this case, the (hoped-for) result, or impact, is well-rounded scholars. But how would we measure that? We'll get into *program evaluation* in more detail in Chapter 5, Evaluation. But a short discussion here will be useful in the meantime.

One way to measure the result would be to survey students' knowledge of the "classics" before the project begins, and again at a later date. Another way would be to compare students' SAT scores before and after the purchase. Or we could track how many students checked out these books, although checking them out wouldn't necessarily correlate with the students' having read them, would it? Therefore, such tally would not be a precise measure of result.

Let's take one more quick example, just to be sure we understand the difference between activity/output and result/impact.

A small clinic in rural Nigeria is almost overwhelmed by the number of people suffering from malaria. They have appealed to you for assistance in obtaining medicine. You have organized a committee to approach drug companies to ask them to donate the needed medications.

The resources here could be persons with high-level contacts, talented writers to create persuasive letters to those contacts, and medical personnel to document the need and assess the kinds of medications required. You would also need funds to ship the medications.

The activities here would be the contacts made, the letters written, the medicines donated, and the donations collected to underwrite the shipping.

The activities at the clinic would be that all those suffering from malaria and coming to our small clinic would receive adequate medical care. The result—the impact—would be a healthier populace.

We have now wrestled these three concepts into a clear relationship. Resources lead to activities that produce results; inputs lead to outputs which generate impact. Results are what we want. Resources and activities are steps along the way.

Exercise 2-3 will help us solidify our understanding of results. Turn to it now, to see how well you have understood this section.

Getting to "Result"

Imagine you are the new president of the newly formed women's club at the over-55 community. Assume that one of the goals of the organization is to improve the community, but no projects have yet been chosen.

Spend a few moments thinking about how you would recommend the club get started. Try to come up with at least five steps the organization should take before it selects a project. You can refer back to the material in Chapter 2 if you need to, but I suspect you can complete this task without doing so if you merely stop and think about it for a few minutes.

_____

_____

_____

_____

_____

_____

_____

_____

_____

_____

This exercise will give you experience in approaching a task from the point of view of the goal rather than the activity or the resources needed to accomplish it.

Starting from the Wrong End

All too often, inexperienced persons focus *only* on resources. They start with what resources they have available, using the resources to lead them into a program. These folks are starting from the wrong end. Instead of starting with an assessment of the needs of the community, then looking at the available resources to determine an appropriate course of action, they start with their resources.

A few hypothetical examples of the inefficiency of starting with the resource:

> ∞ *Example 1: In a small community in Ohio, each high-school junior must complete a community-service project. The initial resources are his time and his creativity. He then goes out to find something to do.*

> ∞ *Example 2: A church outreach committee is allocated a budget of five thousand dollars to give away to local charities in one thousand dollar grants. The resources are the dollars and the committee's time. The committee is restricted by a policy that it can give a grant only to a charity that has a member of the church on its board to act as liaison between the church and the charity. The local charities know this restriction and are careful to be sure they get a church-related member on their board, whether or not that person is even suitable. Meanwhile, some members of the church use this policy to join the most prestigious local boards, without giving a thought to their responsibility to the church's outreach committee.*

> ∞ *Example 3: A Rotary Club plans to host a fundraising golf tournament and invites members to nominate favorite charities to be the beneficiaries. The resources are the time and talent of the tournament committee (the funds raised are a result of the resources—and then become resources themselves). The choice of benefitting charities is based on the personal contact rather than on a response to the biggest problem in the community.* ∞

Note that in each one of these cases, the emphasis has been on the resource—the student's time, the outreach committee's budget, and the Rotary's golf tournament. I call these "resources looking for results." And far too often, this approach results in projects that are half-hearted or inefficient. They have little long-term impact because they usually do not address the most pressing needs in the community.

Not that such resources won't produce some good. The student will undertake a project. The outreach committee will donate the money to local charities. The Rotary will raise some money, likely to be given to the favorite charity of the most vocal or influential members.

So all these programs will have some results of some sort. But will those results address the most important needs in this community?

Starting at the Right End

What if the outreach committee, for example, had taken a different approach? What would their program have looked like if the committee had started by focusing on locating the most dire problem in their community? What if they had identified a critical problem that they wanted to solve? What if they had imagined what the best solution would look like? What if they focused on determining what impact they wanted to achieve with their outreach efforts?

> ∽ *First of all, they needed to know what inputs they could count on regardless of what problem they chose to address. So they surveyed the church population to find out what resources might be available—what talents, skills, expertise, and professions they might draw upon at some future date. Next, they rescinded the policy about church member involvement, realizing that it was an inappropriate restriction.*
>
> *They studied the needs in their community, talked with civic and religious and education leaders, and discovered that the biggest problem in their town was that the children of Spanish-speaking undocumented workers were not getting the necessary childhood inoculations. Further study revealed that the undocumented workers did not understand the need for the inoculations, nor how to have their children inoculated, because no information was available to them in their language. Now the committee knew the problem—untreated children: the cause of the problem—no readily available information; and the solution—an education campaign in Spanish.*

Understanding the ramifications of this situation—sick children, more emergency room visits, more school absenteeism, working mothers losing pay as they stay home to nurse sick children—the committee decided that they would use their entire budget to print informational brochures in Spanish and hire a respected leader of the Hispanic community to distribute them.

The activity here would be the production of the brochures and their distribution to the target audience. The result would be a healthier school population for all children, not just the Hispanics, and reduced child and adult absenteeism.

Note that the outreach committee's consideration of the grant money resource was just one part of their efforts. They did not just write a check and give their money to some local charity. They took the time to investigate local needs, devise a program to deal with a critical one, toted up what resources would be required, and took the steps necessary to solve the situation. They used resources of time, research, investigation, talent, volunteer input, and, yes, their money, to create the Spanish-language literature that would result in the desired result.

They drew upon an impressive panoply of resources. They were wise to first assess all the resources that might be available to them, whatever activity they undertook. Because of that, they already knew they had a public-health nurse who could write an informative brochure. They had members of their congregation who were fully bilingual in Spanish and English who could translate it. They knew a wonderful graphic artist who would volunteer his talents to lay out the brochure and illustrate it. And they knew that the owner of a print-shop was a long-time church member who would print the brochures at a reduced rate. All these resources were available to the committee, saving them money and effort. ∾

By focusing on the problem and what would be needed to solve it, the committee was able to determine which resources would be needed in order to create the necessary activities to achieve that result—that goal.

This discussion may seem somewhat tedious. Let's get on with it, you are probably saying. I can understand your impatience. Some of this seems intuitive, I'm sure. But believe me, more projects have failed, more people have been disappointed and disillusioned, more money wasted, simply because no one took time to answer the question: What is the problem? They hadn't analyzed the situation to decide exactly what they could do to solve it. They hadn't looked at all their options and, through a deliberate process, chosen the best one.

The most common illustration of this backward approach that I see so often is youth or church groups who want to go on a "mission trip." They decide they want to go somewhere to do something. Perhaps they know someone who has been on such a trip and has come back with enticing stories about the wonderful time they had. Frequently they refer to their experience as a "life-changing" event.

But life-changing for whom? They profess to be going somewhere in order to "help." But they merely hop on board an idea and a plane and barge ahead without careful thought as to what problem they want to solve and the best way to solve it.

Well, going there isn't always the answer.

We read recently about a program to take twenty volunteer dentists to the Dominican Republic to provide free dental care for low-income children there. The total cost of the trip was about forty thousand dollars. During the one-week trip the volunteers treated about eight hundred children. That is about eight patients per person per day (assuming a five-day week). And the cost per patient was close to fifty dollars.

For the same forty thousand dollars, the program could underwrite the salary of a local dentist for a year in the Dominican Republic. Assuming that person worked five days a week, fifty weeks a year, and saw only eight patients per day, he, or she, could treat two thousand children a year, at a per patient cost of twenty dollars. Instead of one-shot attention, a local dentist could provide continuing or follow-up care. The patients would likely be more comfortable with a native-Spanish speaker, who could more easily discuss their needs. The dentist would be part of the community, would remain in the community, and might inspire children to consider careers in medicine. Finally, the salary would be spent in the Dominican Republic on housing, food, utilities, and the like, rather than spent on airfares and hotels.

If, rather than taking a week off from work to volunteer in the Dominican Republic, these dentists continued to work at home, and donated their week's salary to the salary of a local medical person, the beneficiaries would be far better off.

This is not to say that mission trips should never be done. Much good has been accomplished around the world by self-less people going to the problem and solving it. But there are really two different kinds of mission trips. We need to be quite sure we know which kind we've chosen. Before we embark on a mission trip, we need to be absolutely sure that we know our objective.

Mission trips to benefit "them"

One possible objective is to provide a service to someone or some group somewhere. We may plan to solve a problem that can't be solved locally for some reason. Well and good. But have we looked closely at alternative ways to accomplish our goal? Is a mission trip really the most effective, most efficient, most sustainable way to achieve our objective? What will be the cost? In money, resources, time? What will be the result? Is our goal the same goal of the people we plan to visit? What "cost" will they incur in hosting our trip? Remember, we will need their time, their expertise, their goodwill. Most needy people around the world are incredibly generous with what little they have; they will provide exceptional hospitality for a visiting "mission group." The cost of such hospitality may seem minimal to us, to them such costs may be significant. Are we aware of what disruption we may cause?

But most of all, we must be positive that the only realistic way to accomplish our goal is to go ourselves on a mission trip.

Sometimes "going there" is undoubtedly helpful, under the right circumstances. This kind of volunteer mission trip meets *a need that cannot be met locally within the necessary time frame*. Helping flood victims shovel mud from their homes is an example. Cleaning up debris after a tornado; providing medical assistance after an earthquake—these need to be done quickly and often require the many hands that make light work.

Here, again, however, we need to address certain key conditions. Ill-equipped volunteers rushing to "help" at a disaster site are what the relief professionals sometimes call "the second disaster." Far too often these volunteers arrive with no forethought as to housing, food, or tools. Immediately they begin to pester the local people or professional disaster specialists with questions: Where can I find a hotel? Where can I get dinner? Do you have a spare [whatever]?

The local people and the professionals are too busy to be able to cater to and care for inexperienced volunteers. So before you rush off on an errand of mercy, be sure your presence and your skills are truly needed. And be sure you will not be a burden to those already over-burdened with responsibilities.

Mission trips to benefit us

This is the second kind of mission trip. There is nothing wrong with such an expedition. It has great benefits. The only downside risk is that we undertake this kind of mission trip in the mistaken notion that we are doing it to benefit "them" instead of us.

Undoubtedly we learn a lot when we go outside our local area to undertake a volunteer task. Whether we spend time on tutoring school children on a Native American reservation in New Mexico or in Mali, Mozambique, or Malaysia, we come away with a new perspective on the world. We learn to appreciate other cultures. We recognize how very fortunate we are. We truly get more than we give.

And that may be the problem. If we approach a mission trip thinking that we are going to be bountiful donors to those greatly in need, answering all their problems, we may be sadly mistaken. Our arrogance will trip us up.

We may find that those we thought we were aiding actually have more to give us than we have to give them. Oh, certainly, we can give them some material goods that they did not have—we can be like Santa Claus in July. (But even that can be fraught with problems, as we have learned, if our gifts replace goods for sale in the local community.)

All too often, those going on volunteer mission trips come back saying, "I got so much more than I gave." Good. But was that the intent?

Better to plan for just that outcome. We need to be sure what our goal is. Is it to benefit "them" or "us"?

One kind of mission trip, then, should be the "Go and see" kind. Go, be with the people. Learn. Absorb the lessons they have to teach us. Be humble and open to learning. Be prepared to *give* your attention, your compassion, your good humor. But be prepared to *receive* more than you give.

So here's a checklist that summarizes some of the above thoughts. Take a moment to run through it. You'll come away far better equipped to deal with the issue the next time someone says, "Let's take a mission trip to….,"

1. What are we trying to accomplish?

2. Who are to be the beneficiaries of this trip?

3. What are we going to do?

4. What do we expect to learn?

5. What is it going to cost?

6. Is there a better way to get the same results?

7. Is there a more effective, long-term way to get the same results?

8. Who could be hurt by this mission trip?

With regard to number eight above, please think carefully about bringing goods that could be purchased locally.

> ∞ *A group of church folks were preparing to go to Cape Town, South Africa, to help expand a residence for AIDS victims. They were well aware that the work could have been done just as easily by hiring local carpenters, and probably for about the same cost as the trip. But they wanted to go, to stand together with those who were suffering—to let them know that people from around the globe cared for them enough to come. They wanted the personal experience of interacting with people from another culture. They wanted to deepen their own understanding of the needs of the less-well-off in South Africa. They wanted to extend their horizons and compassion. They had done their homework and were extremely clear about the purpose of the trip.*
>
> *When the church group met with the South African pastor who was in charge of the residence, they asked him what goods they should bring with them. None of the group had been to Cape Town before; they didn't realize that Cape Town has lovely malls*

and futuristic shops selling every conceivable item. They could purchase anything they needed right there in Cape Town.

The pastor was a wise one, however. He understood the human need to bring something tangible (that's why we take a gift to our hostess at a dinner party). So he suggested that they bring tins of those band-aids for children that are brightly colored with cartoon characters on them. While band-aids were certainly available in Cape Town, the brightly colored ones hadn't made it there yet. ∽

Band-aids aren't expensive, so by bringing some with them, the Americans would not have a significant adverse effect on sales at the local Cape Town stores. Band-aids are easy to transport. And, indeed, I'm sure they brought smiles to the faces of those patients in the residence as they gave the band-aids to their children.

This example illustrates the kind of mission trip of most benefit to all involved. The people going on the trip were undertaking a well-thought-out and managed project under the supervision of a competent local person. They were doing something for a group of people who needed to know that people from far away cared for them.

At the same time, those on the trip recognized that they would probably benefit the most from their experience. They were totally realistic about the goal of their mission trip.

Take one example of the wrong approach just to see the difference.

∽ *A church outreach committee learned about another church's medical mission to Nicaragua. They learned all the details from the organizer of the other mission. "We need to do that," they said. "We'll go to the same place, stay at the same place, and use the same facilities. That will make our planning much easier."*

And so they got a group together, enlisted doctors and nurses they knew in the program, asking them to forego a week of their practice to go on this mission, and raised funds from the congregation to send the delegation. The cost of the trip in out-of-pocket expenses for airfare, hotels, meals, and local transportation amounted to over twenty thousand dollars. The committee estimated that the cost of

*the lost income of the professional participants was probably an
equal amount. So they were proud that this mission trip was valued
at over forty thousand dollars. The committee embarked upon
this program with the goal of mounting a mission trip each year
for at least four years (for a total out-of-pocket cost of over eighty
thousand dollars).* ꙮ

Those who went on the trip did indeed have a "life-changing" experience.
And the Nicaraguans they treated received one week of primary medical
care, which was certainly a benefit. Was the program cost-effective? What
problem was it supposed to address, and did it do so? Was this a lasting
change in the lives of the beneficiaries? (Remember that question as you
read about Sustainability later in this chapter.)

But no one asked the Nicaraguans if they wanted another medical
mission. No one asked them if this was the best use of the Americans'
time and money. No one asked them if the location chosen to set up
the clinic was the best one, or if this group of people were the ones who
most needed the service. (Remember this question as you read about
Partnerships later in this chapter.)

The committee would have had a much smarter program had they started
with an investigation of need—what problem should they undertake to
solve. If they wanted to aid persons in a particular foreign country, they
should have taken the time to learn from those people their most critical
problems. (Medical care might not have been the most pressing issue for
the population in Nicaragua—but no one asked them.)

Once the church group understood the problem, they should have then
investigated what they could do to solve it (one problem might be solved
easily; another might be beyond their means and capabilities). Only then
could they decide if a medical mission trip made sense.

(The goal of the committee might actually have been to provide those
"life-changing" experiences to members of their congregation. That is a
legitimate goal. But if it were the goal, they should not have masked the
effort with the subterfuge of a "helping others" trip. They should have
instead stated their goal clearly and planned activities that would have
supported that goal. That would have been the better way.)

A different better way to good health care might have been obvious if they had included the local people in their investigation. Perhaps rather than spending so much money sending people to Nicaragua each year for four years, they could have found a talented Nicaraguan youth and contributed to the cost of his tuition for four years of medical school. Then the Nicaraguans would have had a local doctor who spoke the language, understood the culture, and would be present year-round for many years to come.

All this illustration proves is that in order to use our resources wisely in the future, let's *start* with our goal—with the impact we want to have—and work our way backwards to activity and resource. We'll have a much greater chance of designing a successful program with real impact. And that would be the better way to do good.

Let me give you one more example of starting from the wrong end.

> ◌ *A women's club was formed in a new over-55 community in a rural, poorer section of the country. The mission of the club was to improve conditions in the existing community surrounding the new development. At the first meeting, the members were asked to propose programs. Some suggested tutoring at the local school. Others suggested volunteering at the hospital. Still others thought they should sponsor an event to raise funds for the local volunteer fire department. After a period of discussion, the members voted for the fundraising event.* ◌

By now you can see the fallacy in these suggestions. All of them focus on activities. No one suggested they form a committee to go out into the community to determine the most glaring problem. None of them suggested canvassing the membership to learn what skills or expertise might be available. No one checked to see if the school, or hospital, or fire department even needed anything before they proposed the activity.

Instead of focusing on the activity, as that committee did, we need to focus on the problem and our desired *result*. Once we have identified the problem and have the potential solution pinned down, we can turn our attention to the various ways we might approach it. The goal and our resource analysis will open our eyes to many possible new options for action. We won't grab the first idea that comes our way. We'll take time to measure how well each option might meet our goal. Often it is not the first idea, or the fifteenth, but the thirty-first idea that turns out to be the best. Brainstorming is a useful tool to find those thirty-one options.

In batting practice, the hitter is instructed "Keep your eye on the ball." That is good advice for anyone embarking on an outreach project. Keep your eye on the result. The resource and the activity are important, but only the result truly matters.

Now take a break from this discussion. Get up and stretch. Then go to Exercise 2-4 at the end of this chapter and spend a few minutes thinking about the questions posed there.

Partnerships

We know that we usually accomplish more when we work in partnership. "Two heads are better than one" is true, and three heads, or four, are often even better. When we work in partnership, we bring more good minds to the task. We bring more experience and expertise. We bring more muscle. In other words, we bring more *resources* to the task.

President Obama's speech at the G-20 meeting on April 2, 2009, made the point that ". . . working in partnership is an excellent beginning [to solving the world's complex problems]. Each of us can bring a portion of the solution so that together, like pieces of a jigsaw puzzle, the various colors and shapes begin to make sense, and then turn into a finished masterpiece. Each piece is important. No piece can be left out without affecting the whole. So each action taken in partnership contributes to the final product."

Furthermore, when we act in partnership, we may uncover obstacles of which we were previously unaware. For example, perhaps we want to address the issue of homelessness in our community. We are impelled to do this because we see families sleeping on the streets or in their cars and wonder why they don't take advantage of the local homeless shelter, just down the street. We've heard that the shelter has empty beds every night.

But when we talk with the homeless, we are told that the shelter turned them away. The shelter has a long-standing policy to house a family no more than three consecutive nights.

No matter what the original rationale was for the policy—and it may have been a good one at the time—the result today is that families are pushed out even when beds are available.

One immediate activity might be, then, to work with the board of directors of the shelter to re-assess that policy in light of current demand.

By working in partnership with the homeless and with shelter management, we uncovered the reason families were not able to access the empty beds. And working in partnership with the board of directors, we may be able to solve this symptom of a greater problem: Why are these families homeless in the first place? We would need to ask that question next. And the homeless and the board of directors would undoubtedly be good partners in solving the problem of homelessness itself.

Caution: Before we form a partnership to solve a problem, we need to know what the problem is and what we expect the solution to look like. A partnership to find a cure for cancer would involve very different people from a partnership to provide school children with a safe after-school program. It would use different resources, would be managed differently, and have a different timeline.

A partnership to ensure adequate nutrition for elderly villagers in Palestine would be very different from a partnership to rebuild the livelihoods of Asian fishermen whose boats were destroyed in the tsunami.

Once again, we must return to our *result determines activity which determines the necessary resources* triad. We need to start with our desired *result*. Once we determine what *activities* will give us that *result*, we can focus on calculating the needed *resources*. And a partnership is, above all, a source of *resources*. A partnership brings needed resources such as money, talent, supplies, expertise, credibility, experience. Just which one or ones of these resources will be useful cannot be determined until we decide what it is that we want to accomplish. Therefore, we must not rush into forming partnerships just because a willing partner is available.

All too often, groups decide that it would be nice to work together. They then cast about looking for something to do. When they find something mutually agreeable they forge ahead, without careful examination of what each partner might bring to the program, what each partner hopes to achieve, and how much or many resources each partner is willing to invest.

A women's volunteer community service organization in a large city entered into a partnership with a major social service organization to build transitional housing for homeless families. Both agreed upon the need; both agreed on the desired activity— a building with 24 apartments and job training for the adult inhabitants—and the desired result—mothers able to provide homes for their children.

What wasn't clearly specified was what resource each partner would provide. While the women's organization thought that it would be involved in all decisions regarding the management of the program, the social service organization saw the women only as funders and providers of job training. As a result, the women's organization was frustrated and concerned over being "ignored"; the social service organization was frustrated at what they perceived as the "meddling" of the volunteers.

Years of acrimony and misunderstanding ensued before the project was finally complete. Only the determination of a few individuals kept the partnership intact to its conclusion. In the meantime, too much time and effort was expended in clarifying roles that should have been explicitly laid out at the beginning of the partnership.

Partnerships are good, but they aren't always necessary. Partnerships for partnership sake rarely work out. The best, the more effective partnerships are established for a specific goal, with clearly defined responsibilities and authorities, and specific timelines agreed upon. All good partnerships have a "sunset" provision, a definite time when the partnership will be dissolved. This gives each partner the opportunity to end its participation without leaving the other in the lurch. It can give a graceful way to end an unproductive or troubled partnership. It also serves to establish a sense of urgency to the partnership. Knowing that a deadline is approaching is a superb motivator—just ask any college student the week before final exams.

So partnerships are important. Partnerships are a tool, a resource. Partnerships are not a goal or an activity. If we keep that in mind, we will enhance our chances for success.

Sustainability

We hear a lot about *sustainability* these days, and we can easily get confused because the word actually is used in two very different contexts. Both are important for us to consider in undertaking an outreach program.

In an environmental context, *sustainability* means that the program will not exhaust natural resources. It means that we should undertake programs to give all human beings a healthy and secure life without consuming the resources of future generations. Any program to reduce poverty today is unsustainable if our actions impoverish our children or grandchildren.

A current worry is the environmental impact of the loss of rain forest in South America. Cutting down the rain forest in Brazil obviously gives peasant farmers more fertile land to farm. But the environmental cost is thought to be incalculable. Future generations will be deprived of the biological diversity to be found in the rain forest, the denuded land will affect rainwater control and flooding. The loss of trees will increase the amount of carbon dioxide in the atmosphere, contributing to global warming. The environment of the entire world will suffer because of the loss of forest land in one area on one continent.

Contrast that unsustainable situation with this sustainable program. Farmers in the Philippines dried their rice on the ground. The rice on the bottom dried slowly because it absorbed moisture from the soil. Some of it rotted as a consequence. Stirring the rice mixed dirt into it. Soil-borne insects infested the rice. Because of these problems, much of the rice had to be discarded, leaving the villagers hungry and suffering from inadequate nutrition.

The problem wasn't the amount of rice being grown, was it?

Rather than tackling the problem by increasing crop yields by fertilizer or creating more arable land, the program implementers simply built 15' x 25' cement drying platforms raised a few inches off the ground. The rice dried far more quickly being lifted away from the moist soil. The rice stayed clean. And fewer insects got into the crop.

As a result, the amount of usable grain increased by over thirty percent—not from increased yield but by preventing waste. This was a sustainable program from an environmental point of view. It was also sustainable in that it continued to provide benefits after the implementers left the scene. That is the second meaning of the word.

Sustainable can also mean that the program can exist on its own after the implementing partners have left. A new school building in Central America that sits empty because the village has no funds to hire a teacher is not a sustainable project. A program to supply solar-powered lights for schools in Africa is not sustainable if the schools cannot obtain new parts and find trained persons in the community to install them. Improving crop yields in the Philippines by providing tractors is not sustainable if the nearest gas station is fifty miles away.

So when we get to the place where we are choosing our project, let's keep in mind both kinds of *sustainable*: environmental considerations *and* the ability to go on even after we have moved on. That's the better way!

Now we need to stop and complete Exercise 2-4 to be sure we have this down pat. Once we feel comfortable, we can forge ahead and start looking at how we will choose our program and what decisions we will have to make. We have now built the foundation for our new and better way of doing good.

Resource, Activity, Result Analysis

Think of a recent project to do good that you participated in.

1. What was the desired result of the project (what problem was it designed to solve)? _____

   _____

   _____

2. What activities led to that result? _____

   _____

   _____

3. What resources were used? _____

   _____

   _____

4. Did you have partners? If so, how were they chosen? _____

   _____

   _____

5. Was the project sustainable in both meanings of the word?

   _____

   _____

6. Looking back now, after our discussion of resources, activities, results, and partnerships, what would you have done differently?

   _____

   _____

7. What results (goals) might you (or your group) be interested in working toward in the next year? (Remember, these are problems to be solved, not activities to be undertaken.) List at least three.

_____

_____

_____

8. Selecting only one of the goals you've named above, list three possible activities that would contribute toward achieving that result, then list three resources that would be needed to support each activity. (Hint: Think of skills, knowledge, products, professional expertise, donated services, real estate, etc.)

	Activity	**Resource**
1.	_____	_____
		_____
		_____
2.	_____	_____
		_____
		_____
3.	_____	_____
		_____
		_____

(Second hint: The same resource [money, for example] might be required for each activity. But each of the activities would undoubtedly require some different mix of resources.)

Summary

We have now looked at a number of terms that are used by development persons: resources, activities, results, partnership, and sustainable. We have noted their particular use in the context of a better way of doing good. We have analyzed the problem. We have understood that we must focus on what we want to achieve, then work backwards to the activities that will produce that result, and finally to the resources that will be needed for those activities. We have seen how starting with finding a use for the resources we have on hand can waste those resources and even bring harm to those we want to aid.

Choices

Lord Ronald flung himself upon his horse
and rode madly off in all directions.

—*Stephen B. Leacock*

Choices, choices. Life is filled with choices. And so is the business of the better way of doing good. So in this chapter we will look at all the possible choices that one must explore when considering an outreach or philanthropic program. These choices will enable us to look at alternatives—to search out all possible routes to our goal. By being sure we have considered all possible choices, we will be able, in Chapter 4, to make the best decision possible.

We long to fix something that we know is wrong in the world. We know that we can't fix everything, but one or two problems seem to us to be especially worthy of our efforts. Maybe we have a personal connection to the problem (a dear relative is suffering from an incurable disease). Maybe we see a danger in our town (the teenagers are hanging around on street corners in the evening because they have no place to go). We may have read about a particular problem that calls upon our particular expertise. (If you are a teacher, you might be concerned that elementary schools are closing in Africa. The schools lack local teachers because the teachers are emigrating to places with higher-paying jobs).

Whatever the predicament, we long to find a remedy that is meaningful, appropriate, culturally sensitive, and rewarding to all parties. (We also want it to be easy, low cost, and quick, don't we?) So we want to get started. We feel ready.

We understand the basics of good development work, because we paid attention to the points in Chapter 2. We have enthusiasm and excitement. "Bring it on! We're rarin' to go!"

Whoa there. Hold on for just a moment. As we have learned, far too often, individuals or groups jump into a program wholeheartedly, well-intentioned, but with little forethought. Then they are surprised when they achieve less-than-optimum, and sometimes disastrous, results. First is not always best. Better to slow down, do our homework, get our ducks in order. As we have found out, there is a better process that will lead to better results. That better process is called strategy.

Better to take our time to find the right line of attack rather than be the first out of the gate and crash. The less preparation we make, the greater likelihood that we will fail, that we will be disappointed and disillusioned. We might be discouraged from trying again. We might be tempted to agree with Mark Twain, who said "No good deed goes unpunished." (Incidentally, Twain got it wrong because he focused only on the activity, not the result. A good deed, done in the right way at the right time with the right partners, addressing the right problem, will almost always be rewarded.)

The number of choices facing us is far greater than apparent at first glance. That's always the case when we embark on a new project or undertaking. If we decide to take a cruise, we are faced with myriad choices: where to sail, when, on what ship, at what price, with whom. If we are heading off to college, we have to choose where to go, where to live, what courses to take, which professors to avoid, how to make new friends, and how to pay for it. If we are stuck in a dead-end career, we need to choose how to make a move, and when, and to what other occupation, and with what other company, or whether to strike out on our own, and at what cost.

Choices face us every day, in everything that we do. Why should we think that it would be any different when we want to do good? We still have lots and lots of choices to make. And until we examine all those choices, we should not attempt to come to any decisions. Until we have examined the full range of our options, we shouldn't settle on any one of them.

When we complete an inventory of all the alternatives we might undertake to solve a problem, we will be prepared to make the best possible choice. And if we choose the right problem, choose the right method of fixing the problem, choose the right resources and the right activities, and collaborate with the right partners, we greatly enhance our chances of success.

Choosing the right problem is the first step. But how do we do that? Generally, I believe in the saying, "The process is not the point." All too often, well-meaning groups become so entrenched in the *process* of choosing that they lose sight of the point. They spin their wheels instead of moving on. They fuss and fritter away at the edges of the problem, never getting down to the crux of the issue.

In this case of choosing what problem we are going to address, however, the process *is* the point. Note that the process is *only* to lead us through the many choices we have to make to arrive at the best program, which we will then implement. The whole process of choosing should be done as quickly as possible. Time squandered in process doesn't result in change. Time wasted is time lost. It dilutes our resources.

Unfortunately, just any old road will not lead us to success in this venture. Only the right road will deliver us and our assistance to those in need, at the least waste of resources, in the most timely way, and to the ultimate benefit of all participants, especially the recipients of our services. We need a map to guide us from the starting point of the urge to reach out. We need a map that shows us the right highway to our destination, preventing us from dead-end detours. Such a map will clearly point out the road signs and checkpoints along the way.

Fortunately, a simple clear map does exist. We've already examined the A(pproach) and the (B)asics in Chapters 1 and 2. Now we're at the (C)hoices step. Now we're going to describe a methodical, step-by-step procedure that will give you, or your group, a map with sufficient detail to make your journey pleasant and productive.

Choosing Your Role in Doing Good

Before you can select the target population, you need to make one key determination. The first choice you need to make is your role. The first question is whether you (or your group) are an investor, an intermediary, an implementer, or an innovator. So we're all on the same page, let's define each of these terms in the context of outreach.

What is your role?

The following definitions are necessarily, even arbitrarily, narrow. For the time-being, we're going to be as overly precise as we can be about our meanings. So don't be tempted, at this point, to second-guess me with, "Well, but couldn't an investor also be an implementer?" Sure, but we need to understand each term on its own before we start synthesizing. Later on, we'll combine some of these categories, as we know that many people engage in more than one of these functions. Some people might be investor-implementers or innovators-investors. I suppose someone could be a triple-threat: innovator-investor-implementer. But until we get to that point, let's keep these categories separate.

Here, then, are our definitions:

An *investor* provides resources (money, time, talent, etc.) to an ongoing program. The simplest form of investing is just writing a check and sending it off to some philanthropic venture. Or, in today's world, someone who simply clicks on the "Donate Now" button on a website. These contributors provide resources but take no part in decision making or operations. This type of investor is the least *personally* involved in the endeavor.

Investor

I don't want anyone to mistake me here. I don't want you to think that I believe that those who take on the role as financial investors are not important. In fact, without investors, nothing would get started, nothing would get done. Investors provide the resources that enable development programs. Investors such as Bill Gates have had enormous impact—they have underwritten impressive and extensive programs, particularly in health in Africa. Thousands, if not millions, of people's lives have been improved because of the grants of the Gates Foundation.

And so investing in organizations that undertake the kind of work you want to support is important. And contributing money certainly is easier. Absent any other activity, writing a check is at least a step in the right direction.

But here, too, care should be given to the approach. More on this later.

Intermediary

An *intermediary* acts as a bridge between an investor and the program implementers. The intermediary is most often formed to support another organization, such as the alumni associations of universities. The intermediary may be a separate not-for-profit organization whose sole purpose is to raise funds for a particular cause, such as the NAACP's Legal Defense Fund. Colleges and universities establish alumni foundations to raise money to underwrite athletic programs (the alumni who contribute to these foundations are, of course, investors once-removed).

The intermediary might be a church-related outreach group or the philanthropy committee of the local Rotary Club. Such groups receive money from their principals (the church congregation or the Rotary Club itself) and turn around and donate it to other organizations. In most of these cases, these groups do not intend to undertake any direct action; they plan to serve only as conduits for monetary donations to other causes.

That is not to downplay their importance. They are *very* important. At the very least, the good ones serve as a convenient, safe channel for investors to direct their resources with confidence. (In these two cases, the "investors" would be the members of the church congregation or the Rotary Club.) The good intermediaries serve a promotional and educational function, bringing problems to the attention of those with the resources to devote to their solution. The good intermediaries provide resources so the implementers can undertake projects and programs. The activities of the intermediaries make possible the work of the implementers. Intermediaries are vitally important and should be considered key partners in development and relief work.

Implementer

The *implementers* actually do the hands-on work. They do the day-to-day program design, implementation, monitoring, and evaluation. They receive the resources provided by the investors, sometimes via an intermediary, as we discussed above. They translate those resources into sustainable, effective programs. Very often, the implementers are paid, professional staff working for a development or social service organization. They carry out the work of the agency. They manage the programs. They do the work. They collect information on successes and disappointments. They report to the investors and the intermediaries.

The successful implementers focus on one problem in their area, or a group of similar problems, and work to alleviate them. Even the smallest local agencies are involved in implementing their programs in order to solve the target problem.

Let's look at a few examples of implementers.

Almost every community has a food pantry. The Boy Scouts, or churches, or social service organizations such as the Lions Club may hold food drives to stock the shelves of the food pantry. The food pantry is an important asset to any community. The food pantry serves to implement the community's response to hunger among its citizens. It focuses on families who are experiencing hard times. It serves as a bridge between those who have plenty to eat and those whose cupboards are bare.

A few local organizations are designed to enhance the educational experience of the school children. PTAs undertake a variety of programs in support of school activities. The Friends of the public library may tutor middle-school students who are falling behind in their English classes.

A Junior League typically assesses need in its hometown and then chooses a partner among the other community agencies that is dedicated to meeting those needs. The partners together refine and document the goal, set up the framework, design the interventions, and plan the work. The League volunteers roll up their sleeves and contribute hands-on work and leadership skills to implement the programs.

All these organizations do a fine job as implementers.

The *innovators*, whether individuals or organizations, dream up new ways to solve problems. Maybe they find new agricultural methods. Maybe they design new vaccines. Maybe they create online literacy programs that can be downloaded onto solar-powered laptops in regions too remote for electricity.

Innovators

An innovator is an inventor. An innovator sees a problem, sees that the current solutions aren't working, and devises a whole new approach. The innovator isn't constrained by "what we've always done" or "we've never done that before." The innovator isn't bound by preconceived ideas of appropriateness or suitable methods. The innovator takes a fresh look at the problem from a new vantage point and creates a new solution. Very often the innovator must also be a "salesman" for his or her idea—new ideas sometimes run into the "we've never done that before" mindset.

An innovator's remedy is useless, of course, unless an investor is convinced to provide the necessary resources and an implementer actually puts the remedy to work.

Some Special Considerations about the Investor Role

And if you are asking for money you should answer these for your investors

If you are considering a donation or contribution to some organization or cause, you should follow some of the same steps we have outlined above. You should mentally run through the resource/activity/goal formula. What do you want to achieve with your check, with your donation? Do you want to contribute to a cause, such as landmine prevention or cancer cures? Do you want to support the work of a local charity that addresses a local need? Do you want to be counted among those movers and shakers supporting a local cultural or civic resource—maybe the symphony or the hospital? Do you want to increase your charitable giving to lower your taxes?

Knowing what you want to achieve will guide you in giving away your money. What you want to do is practice good "grantsmanship." Many, many excellent books have been written for would-be donors. Several of them are listed in the bibliography. We certainly agree that monetary resources are vitally important. Therefore we are going to sketch briefly in this chapter some of the considerations one should make when considering a donation of money.

In other words, there is a Better Way of Doing Good, even when you write a check.

Sometimes a cash gift to some nonprofit organization is the only thing that we are able to do to address a specific problem. Sometimes a gift of money is the best thing to do (in the case of a tragic natural disaster, such as a hurricane, for example). Particularly in the case of emergencies, donations by cash or check are usually needed immediately. Whether the emergency situation is the result of natural forces such as earthquakes or floods, or civil emergencies such as wars, relief agencies need quick funding to provide food, water, emergency shelter, and medical care. In those cases, we all should dig deep in our pockets and contribute (but only to respected and well-known disaster-response agencies).

But do respond and do so wisely. Such gifts are important and needed. ✓

For some reason, gifts from individuals are usually called donations or contributions, while gifts from groups such as foundations, outreach or philanthropy committees, corporations, etc., are usually called grants. However, the process of making such gifts is usually called grantsmanship, regardless of the kind of entity making the gift.

So in this section, we're going to talk about grantsmanship. What we have to say applies equally to individuals and groups. If you are an individual with only a small amount to give away each year, you will want to practice good grantsmanship to be sure that your precious dollars are going as far as they possibly can. If you are part of a group, you have a "fiduciary duty" to be sure that the funds of that group are used efficiently. You will want to practice good grantsmanship as a way of ensuring effective oversight.

A colleague of mine once commented rather facetiously that the best advice he could give someone contemplating making a grant was "Don't." What he meant was that most people make grants for the wrong reason or in the wrong way. They give their money away with little forethought or research. They donate here, and there, in small amounts. They don't really know what the recipient organization does, or how, or most importantly, how well. They do not follow the simple precepts of good grantsmanship.

Certainly we all start with good intentions. But good intentions alone can lead to wasted resources. Did we see a problem and intend to do something about it? Did we then get so busy that we just quickly made a donation to some group involved in the cause, hoping some good came of our cash? Did we rely on a friend's personal appeal or some organization's heart-rending written solicitation? Did we just send them a check hoping that they had more than just good intentions—that they had good programs?

Frankly, these don't seem to be very good reasons to part with my money, and I'm sure they don't seem so to you, either.

When I first took over a tired sixty-year-old relief and development organization supported by donations, I realized that our message to our donors was, "Give us some of your money, and we'll find something good to do with it." And people had done just that. For sixty years they had just sent in their money.

Then people had started to ask, "Why should I give you my money? I can find something good to do with it myself. I don't need you." And contributors started falling away, slowly, year after year.

What distressed me even more than the message we were sending to our donors, however, was that our donors were not holding us accountable. Our well-intentioned donors gave us their money . . . and never asked us what happened to it—or what difference it had made. No one asked to see our financial statements. We issued an annual report that listed to whom we had made grants, and for what purpose. We had not followed up to find out how those grants were used—for the purpose we had funded, or some other purpose?

Such "hands-off" philanthropy was once more or less standard procedure. Individuals, and smaller groups, had little opportunity to learn more about the organizations that they wanted to fund. Sending in a check was just about the only way that the average person (or small group) could participate in good works. The hands-off approach was their only option. Of course, big foundations had staff to do the necessary research and follow-up. But for a small donor to do so would have been extremely cumbersome and difficult.

Not too long ago—before the Internet—small donors had to work hard to find out what an organization actually did (rather than what its fundraising pitch focused on), who was on its board, what its budget was, and where and how it worked. So they had to trust. And in most cases, it is true, that trust was earned. But once in a while—even a few times would be too often—that trust was misplaced. Either the organization didn't do what it said it was going to do, or it didn't do as much as it said, or worst of all—hadn't actually accomplished anything at all.

We are incensed when we learn that government aid programs have been wasteful or ineffective. *USA Today* for March 31, 2009, reported that we had "little to show for billions spent on Afghans" and quoted Secretary of State Hilary Clinton that "We're going to . . . trace the investment and the payoff for the American taxpayer . . . . [I]t's heartbreaking . . . the amount of money that was spent . . . and the failure of being able to produce results that people can point to."

If we are upset about the waste of our tax dollars, shouldn't we get equally distressed about a waste of our donated dollars (and time and energy and talent)?

Stop and think about the last few times you gave a contribution to some good cause. Did you later check to see what had been achieved with your dollars (combined with those of others, of course)? If so, good for you. You are among the very few who do. But most of us don't really focus on measuring *results*, do we? We give money to the annual fundraising appeal from the local homeless shelter without investigating how well they are serving the homeless. We don't follow up to see how it used the money it received. We don't ask the managers what they have accomplished and what difference they have made because of it.

More to the point, do we find out if we should support that shelter in the first place? Is it more efficient than other shelters, or not? How many people is it serving, and at what per-client cost? Are its costs too high? Not enough to truly make a difference? (Either is equally possible.) Is it evaluated by an independent agency such as a community fund? Is a shelter the answer to homelessness in our community, or is there a better way to solve this problem?

To practice good grantsmanship, you will not want to make monetary donations to any organization until you are convinced that it is doing the right thing for the right people at the right time. We should never respond without serious inquiry to appeals from groups that we have never heard of. Unscrupulous people can be found everywhere, particularly in situations where our heart strings are plucked. That is a perfect opportunity for them to pickpocket our wallets.

We contribute to our church (or mosque or synagogue) to underwrite its operating cost, but how many of us ever look carefully at the annual report to see how well it has accomplished its stated mission. Most annual reports are a compilation of activities, with no information about results.

We give to a breast cancer research organization, but how many of us know what it does and how it differs from the other organizations tackling the same illness? Is our organization duplicating some other organization's work? Do we evaluate its results?

We give to our local non-profit hospital, but do we know its ratio of earned to donated income? Do we know what its mortality rate is compared to other hospitals in the region? If we gave for a specific service (well-baby care), do we ask how many patients were seen and at what cost?

These kinds of questions are part of practicing good grantsmanship. Asking them will help us maximize the impact of our donation. Asking them will also encourage the recipient agency to be more pro-active in presenting complete information to its donors. So you will be doing yourself—and all other donors—a great service.

So we agree that practicing good grantsmanship has many important benefits. But exactly how do we go about it?

To sketch the basic steps of good grantsmanship, we're going to reiterate the steps you've learned in the preceding chapters about outreach work. They work equally well when you are considering a monetary donation or a grant.

To practice good grantsmanship, we follow exactly the same process that we would if we were to engage in a hands-on program. We start with the same basic precepts. We keep to the same format. We work through the steps just as we have done so far. Let's review how those segments would be put into play if we were going to make a grant.

Just as we should never approach outreach by thinking of *who* we are going to "help" rather than *what problem* we're going to solve, we should never support an organization (who), rather than a cause (what problem).

That concept is so important that we want to repeat it again:

> *We should never support an organization,*
> *rather than a cause.*

If you want to support the "cause" of breast cancer research, then find the organization doing the best job. Start with the "what"—the problem—rather than the "who"—the organization. Don't just give to the first appeal that comes in the mailbox. Don't give to an organization just because you saw its advertisement on TV. Don't give to something just because your neighbor is involved. Please don't give to something just because a celebrity endorses it unless you are positive that the celebrity is very well informed about the issue.

If you really want your donation to make a difference, in this case to support research into prevention of breast cancer, then invest a bit of time investigating all the organizations dedicated to its eradication. Find out what they do, who supports them, how they operate, and what their track record is. Look at their annual report. Check out their website. You're looking for the one that is making the biggest difference. You are also looking for something that seems amiss. Does anything there beep your skepticism monitor? If so, beware. Follow your instincts, and if your instinct tells you something seems fishy, be sure you reel in that line and investigate the bait.

One simple mistake people often make is to neglect to ascertain that the organization they want to support has a 501(c)(3) tax-exempt status—and in its own name. Usually the organization does. But you should be sure. Sometimes it does not.

> ∽ Several years ago an organization with an extremely important-sounding mission—let's call it "Solar Cookers for Andean Villages" (SCAV)—was soliciting funds from various church groups. The organization had raised quite a bit of money. Only when one potential funder started asking some tough questions did the organization reveal that, yes, they had a tax-exempt ruling, but the ruling applied to the family's philanthropic foundation, not for Solar Cookers for Andean Villages. All contributions were to be made payable to SCAV but deposited in the family foundation's bank account. They said the family foundation would use the money for the mission described.
>
> Solar Cookers for Andean Villages was not itself a legal organization. It had never incorporated and had no tax-exempt status. Therefore,

the so-called "board of directors" of the program was not, in fact, a legally constituted body nor did it have any legal oversight. Moreover, members of the small "board" were the family patriarch, his son, the supplier of the solar cookers, a spokesperson for the program whose expenses were paid by the program, and a couple of other persons.

The skeptical donor inquired why the organization had not incorporated itself. "We haven't gotten around to it," was the response.

The prospective donor declined to contribute because 1) the organization did not legally exist; 2) an organization that couldn't "get around" to this most basic organizational procedure might also be shortchanging other vital administrative functions, such as financial controls and auditing; 3) there were too many "insiders" on the purported board of directors.. ∾

This example points out the necessity of being sure you do the necessary "due diligence" investigation to be sure everything is in place. As we said, almost always it is. Don't think we are casting aspersions on every non-profit out there, or even most of them. We are certain that almost all of them operate entirely on the up-and-up. But you don't want to be caught in the rare instance when not all information is revealed correctly.

A common place for such "stretching" the truth is when people attend some kind of meeting—maybe in someone's home, maybe at church or at a meeting of their civic association. The speaker is dynamic, charming, and tells a heart-rending but inspiring story. The audience gets caught up in the moment. Someone suggests taking up a donation. Men get out their wallets. Women dig deep in their purses. Some pull out checkbooks.

But does anyone say, "Thank you for coming, but I think I'll research this a bit more before I part with some of my cash"? Wouldn't the others look at that person as a curmudgeon? Tightfisted? Persnickity?

But that answer is exactly the right one.

Remember the Music Man? Remember the side-show barkers? Remember the snake-oil salesmen? They inhabit the charitable field just as they do anywhere else.

Beware.

Ask two simple questions: What problem are you trying to solve? What success have you had?

Don't be satisfied with half-answers. Don't be satisfied with "I was there and saw for myself." Don't be satisfied with "Everyone says. . . ."

Ask for facts. Ask what measurements they make before their program begins and afterwards. Ask who evaluates their program. Now please don't misunderstand. We are not saying that all, or some, or even a very small percentage of these folks are charlatans. We'd be surprised if even a tiny portion of them even came close to being a con artist. So we're not so worried about those who set out to swindle us.

We are concerned about those who prey on our sympathy to raise money for good causes—but use that money in ways that are less effective, less efficient, less productive than we would hope. We simply do not need to support organizations that do not adhere to the highest standards and accomplish the best work.

Many donors believe that if they contribute a ten dollar check to an organization, that organization now has another ten dollars to spend on its programs. That is not true. Part of that dollar must go to paying for the good management of that donation.

At a minimum, the organization has to pay the bank fee for processing that donated check, must write and mail a thank you letter to the donor, and account for the income on its financial records.

> ❧ *In the mid-1990s, a very large not-for-profit hospital was engaged in a major capital fund-raising drive. The accounting department was concerned about the cost of processing small donations, so they calculated exactly how much it cost to handle a donation in the form of a check. Including the staff time to record the contribution, deposit it in the bank, send a thank-you letter to the donor, and pay the various out-of-pocket costs such as postage, they calculated that each contribution actually cost the hospital just over twenty-seven dollars. It was losing money on each donation for less than that.* ❧

Nothing about their process of handling donations was significantly different from that of any other non-profit organization.

As a result of this analysis, the fundraising department of the hospital stopped soliciting very small donations and concentrated on approaching individuals and foundations with the capacity to give larger gifts.

Those who don't understand this very real consequence of their giving habits can inadvertently cause organizations actually to lose money. An older woman in New York City thought that she was extremely charitable. She donated to myriad causes, and let people know how philanthropic she was. She would say: "Every time I get an appeal I send a check for twenty five dollars. We can't afford to be big philanthropists, but we can do our part."

She truly believed that she was making a difference with her twenty-five dollar checks. But what was the recipient organization getting out of it? Her twenty-five dollar donations were probably costing the benefitting organizations more than they were gaining.

Furthermore, by contributing to everything that came her way, she wasn't doing her "due diligence" about the organizations she was supporting.

Another major mistake donors sometimes make is to think that money spent on salaries or administration is not as important as money spent on programs. Donors somehow think that an organization that spends only three percent, or six percent, or some other small percentage of their funds, on administration is "better" than organizations that spend more. This is simply untrue.

Administrative costs are necessary costs. We want to know that someone reliable is in charge. We want to know that the financial books are being kept properly. We want to be kept up to date about the work of the organization through regular and informative communications. Those administrative functions are absolutely vital to the effective operation of the charity.

Every contribution carries an inherent cost (even a cash donation requires the time of someone to count it, account for it, deposit it). We want the organization to keep good records. We want the organization to thank us for our gift and provide us with a valid tax-deduction receipt. We want the organization to be run by experienced staff. We want the books to be audited. We want an annual report. We want the board to meet regularly and oversee the operations of the charity. We want to be able to go to the website and check out the latest news from "our" charity.

All this costs money. All the costs of the charity—whether for direct service, for program supplies, for salaries, for auditors, for staff, for paper and pencils and computers—are vital to the mission of the organization. All are "good" costs. None of them can be omitted if the organization is to be well—and efficiently—run. In other words, we want someone minding the store and letting us know about it. In sum, administrative costs are an integral part of the organization's mission. After all, the word "minister" is right in the middle of administration.

An organization that claims an incredibly low cost of administration may be able to conduct its work properly at such a low cost, but in general, we do well to be skeptical. The organization may be skimping on the necessary support services. It may not have enough staff "minding the store." It may not be keeping accurate and complete financial records. It may not be paying mandated employee taxes.

Or it may be presenting incomplete information. It may not be counting all its costs (some organizations that enjoy donated office space do not count as an imputed expense what they would have spent on rent). It may be inflating the value of donated products. There may be many other suspicious reasons why it has such a low administrative cost. Watch for them.

A few charities have misled the public for years by promising that "Every dollar you give will go to our programs." Some even claim (and many still do) that your contribution goes "one hundred percent to program, since our administrative costs are paid for by others." Charities that set up a clash between "good" contributions (those that go to program) and "bad" contributions (those that go to administrative functions) are misleading the public.

When a donor restricts a contribution to be used only for direct program costs, the organization has to pay the connected administrative costs with money from somewhere else. Generally it pays those costs out of the money donated by others who have not placed such restrictions on their gifts—so called "unrestricted" contributions. Donors of unrestricted contributions are charged twice, then—first, to pay for the administrative costs of their own gifts and again to pay for the administrative costs of the restricted gift. This is clearly unfair to the donors of unrestricted gifts.

Donors certainly can restrict donations to a particular geographic area, a program sector (health, education), or even to a specific program of the benefitting organization. Some contributors restrict their donation to a specific portion of the budget of a program. Someone might underwrite the cost of the textbooks for an English as a Second Language Course, for example. Such restrictions are quite legitimate and acceptable.

In these cases, the recipient organization should still have a publicly stated policy that it will deduct from restricted contributions the standard administrative cost of processing those donations. We've never yet met a donor who refused to make a gift so long as this policy was clearly stated.

No, legitimate restrictions are fine. It is the unreasonable restrictions, such as "None of this contribution can be used for administrative costs," that are objectionable.

Some people mistakenly dictate that none of their contribution can be spent on salaries. Now that is just plain silly. Imagine a school that paid no salaries. No salaries equals no teachers. Imagine a hospital that paid no salaries. No salaries equals no doctors or nurses. Imagine a major symphony orchestra that paid no salaries. No salaries equals no musicians or conductors. Salaries aren't money down the drain. Salaries are people doing the work. Such restrictions are well-meaning but misguided.

So some administrative costs are necessary. Most organizations keep their administrative costs below twenty percent. On its website, the American Institute of Philanthropy discusses the "reasonable" percent spent on charitable purpose: "This is the portion of total expenses that is spent on charitable programs. In AIP's view, sixty percent or greater spent on program is reasonable for most charities. The remaining amount is spent on fundraising and administration."

The value of a charity is not how much it spends on what. The value of a charity is what it accomplishes. Think about it. Do you want to judge an organization by looking at its budget, or by looking at what it achieves?

Organizations that operate primarily what are called "gifts-in-kind" programs will usually have administrative costs that appear very low. They are able to do this because of the value of the products that they receive. They provide an effective conduit for surplus or unneeded goods—transferring them from donor to those who need the goods.

Be sure you look behind the administrative-program ratio of organizations that accept gifts-in-kind. Many of them provide incredibly vital supplies, such as medications and tents for the survivors of earthquakes or hurricanes and food and water for families displaced by civil conflict. These goods are frequently life-saving.

However, estimating the dollar value of those gifts is an art, not a science. Most of those agencies are ethical and careful with their numbers. A few, however, have been known to inflate their appraisal of donated goods or to accept at full retail cost goods of questionable worth, such as outdated medicines. This estimating system allows them to claim an exceptionally high program-to-administrative-cost ratio. For a donor to rely simply on the stated ratio ("Our administrative costs are only two percent.") without looking behind the numbers would be foolish. Perhaps the valuation is correct. If so, great. But check first.

Even if the dollar valuation is accurate, the gifts may not be of much benefit to the recipients. Remember the arctic-weight sleeping bags and high-heeled shoes sent to victims of the earthquakes in hot and rocky El Salvador mentioned earlier? Neither of these gifts was useful to people whose homes were in rubble and whose livelihoods had disappeared. But the organization claimed that it had distributed thousands of dollars of assistance to the Salvadorans. The Salvadorans felt that they had gotten lots of stuff of very little consequence. And because the organization placed a high monetary value on the sleeping bags and high-heeled shoes, they could claim their aid was provided at an extremely low administrative cost.

To repeat: Most organizations that provide gifts-in-kind provide a great and needed service. Check them out just as carefully as you would check out any other organization. Do not determine the effectiveness of a charity by looking at its administrative costs. That is only one consideration, and a minor one. We don't judge an organization simply by looking at a ratio. We judge it by what it does. Look instead at what it actually accomplishes. That's our simple message here.

Many, many organizations out there are exemplary. Find those and support them. Give them your money. Let them use it to solve problems.

If you are interested in one particular situation, you can direct your money by making a "restricted contribution." Please, however, don't over-designate your gift. That drives organizations crazy. Don't designate your gift only for planting one specific kind of zinnia in one specific area of a community garden on one specific day—an example that is bit overblown, we admit, but not too far off the mark of some designations we've heard of.

> ∾ *A woman was interested in underwriting a professorship in trauma response at a major university hospital. She wanted the designation to be for research into trauma experienced after date-rape because of an incident in her family. The hospital would have refused the one million five hundred thousand dollar gift under those terms; it considered the terms too restrictive. By talking with the donor, however, the hospital showed the donor the wisdom of a less-restrictive designation. She made the gift for a professorship in trauma.*
>
> *She also made a condition of the gift that the hospital report to her when they filled the professorship position and send her an annual report of the funds in the professorship account for the following ten years. The hospital was pleased to comply with this restriction.* ∾

On the other hand, Yale University recently returned a large contribution designated for a professorship because the donor wanted input into the selection of the person to hold the position. Yale rightly saw this restriction as inappropriate.

Designating your gift is one way to exert a bit of control over your contribution. Your money is important. Your money can do much good in the world. Just find the right program, run by professionals who know what the problem is, have clearly done their homework, and are detail-oriented. You want an implementing partner who is effective and efficient.

Don't waste your money. So much needs to be done in the world, we can't afford to waste money on ineffective programs.

Even if you aren't wealthy, your contributions are vital.

Give what you can, but give wisely. Remember to give only to well-run organizations dedicated to solving a problem. Remember that very small contributions (generally those under twenty five dollars) often cost the organization more than they are worth to it.

The one exception to this is online donations. Since these are handled in cyberspace, with acknowledgements generated by the computer and the funds transferred electronically from one bank account to another, the cost is significantly less. Charities are discovering that at virtually no cost they can send thousands of e-mail solicitations to their donor lists at regular intervals. And those donors are generally pleased to receive frequent reports from the organizations they support.

That's why so many organizations have beefed up their online donation programs—and those that have not are missing the boat.

Not only are such programs low-cost, they frequently encourage larger or more regular gifts. Churches are discovering that allowing donors to set up automatic withdrawals from their checking accounts results in a higher percentage of pledge fulfillment. Some churches have actually installed ATMs just inside the front door to encourage spur of the moment contributions. Charities that are not taking advantage of all the technology available today are deliberately foregoing resources they could easily capture. They are nineteenth century charities ignoring the twenty-first century world. And do you want to give your money to nineteenth century charities or those not taking advantage of the technology now available?

So many considerations. We know there is a lot to take into account. That's why we've tried to make this as simple as possible for you. If you want to make a grant or a donation, simply follow all the steps outlined in this book. You'll find they will guide you to Doing Good the Better Way, regardless of the resources you have to give.

And remember that giving money the Better Way is a centuries-old dilemma.

> ∞ *Aristotle once said, "To give away money is an easy matter . . . and in any man's power. But to decide to whom to give it, and how large and when, for what purpose and how, is neither in every man's power nor an easy matter. Hence it is that such excellence is rare, praiseworthy, and noble."* ∞

At this point, don't forget that money is only one of the many resources—the many inputs—we might devote to solving a problem. Those who provide their contacts, or their skills, or an unused piece of property are also investors. Anyone who provides a resource is an investor.

Of course, investors might fulfill additional roles, as we mentioned above. For example, an *investor* in a for-profit company might also run the company, be an employee, or sit on its board. For our purposes, however, we are restricting investing to mean *only* the provision of resources, with no management, decision-making, or oversight implications.

Choosing the Right Fit

Now that we have looked into the difference between these four categories of persons engaged in solving problems, we need to find out where we fit. Whether you are reading this book alone, or whether you are part of a committee or task force, you need to choose which category best fits you or your group. Exercise 3-1 will help you do that.

If you are part of a group, each member should, individually, fill out a copy of this exercise—then the entire group should discuss each point. *Each member* must participate in order for the discussion to be meaningful. You want to be very careful that everyone agrees with your assessment. If some of you see your role as implementers, and others choose only to be investors, you have a dilemma right at the outset. Better to be sure you are all on the same page before you begin writing your program design. So turn to Exercise 3-1 on the next page and have some fun with it.

Innovator, Investor, Intermediary, or Implementer

This is just a quick little quiz to help you discover which approach to outreach best fits you. Answer the following questions as honestly as you can, for yourself alone. (If you are a member of a group, each person should fill out the quiz personally before the group compares its findings.) There are no right or wrong answers, and you will probably find that your answers fall into a couple of categories. That's OK—we're looking for guidance here, not hard and fast rules.

1. A neighboring community was flooded when a river dike broke. Would you rather

   a) write a check to the Red Cross,

   b) volunteer at the Red Cross to answer phones about where people can send contributions,

   c) work in flooded homes shoveling out mud, or

   d) investigate why the dike failed?

2. A Muslim woman in Malaysia has been sentenced to caning for drinking beer. Would you rather

   a) make an online donation to a women's rights' organization,

   b) sign a protest petition to be sent to the Malaysian government,

   c) set up a meeting with the Malaysian delegate to the United Nations to convey your concern over the sentence, or

   d) organize a group to study Islam to better understand its proscriptions.

3. A small community in Bosnia has found an unusual disease among its dairy cattle that renders the milk unfit for the children to drink. Would you rather

   a) send a donation to a private rural development agency that will replace the herds,

   b) encourage the U.S. Department of Agriculture to get involved to prevent the spread of the disease,

   c) organize a group of volunteer veterinarians to go to Bosnia, or

   d) investigate whether the Bosnians could grow soy beans and process them into soy milk?

RESULTS: Add up the number of answers for

   a) _____

   b) _____

   c) _____

   d) _____

If you had mostly a) answers, you are an investor. You recognize the need to be involved and to be part of the solution, but you would rather give of your resources than of your time or your talent. That's fine. Resources are needed.

If you had mostly b) answers, you are an intermediary. You enjoy putting together people with resources with folks who can use them. You function as a bridge, and bridges are essential when we want to cross a raging torrent.

If you had mostly c) answers, you are an implementer. You like the hands-on work. You want to be personally engaged in the process. You get satisfaction from being on-site and seeing the work progress.

Finally, if you had mostly d) answers, you are an innovator. While you care deeply about the current crisis, you are more interested in preventing its happening again, or finding alternative solutions to the problem. This approach is more theoretical than the others, but it is equally valuable as it is the source of our new ideas and new approaches to old problems.

If you are part of a group, you should now tally your findings. Undoubtedly you will find some members fall into each category. That's a good thing, for when we get to looking at the various options for addressing a problem, we will have the benefit of a variety of approaches.

On the other hand, if the majority of your group fall squarely in one category or another, you should take that finding very seriously. If ninety percent of you are investors, you probably would be wise to avoid planning a hands-on implementer project. If most of you are innovators, you are going to be very unhappy cast in the role of intermediary.

Put this exercise aside, for now, but remember the results. They will be important.

Choosing the Group Process toward Decision Making

Too often a decision to embark on an outreach or charitable program is made by a few, usually self-nominated, individuals. For our process to work, however, every member of the involved group must understand, endorse, and fully support the idea to undertake some sort of philanthropic action (this is true whether or not each person will ultimately be personally involved in deciding which program to initiate or in actually carrying out the work). Therefore, each member must participate in the decision making. Ownership and commitment begin here.

In classic development work, this is called the "Participatory Community" process (more about that to follow), and that is what we are trying to achieve here. Your group is the "community" that is undertaking this first step—the decision to engage in some as-yet undefined outreach project.

While you decide to go ahead with some program (you haven't yet decided which one), you will bring other people into your "community." Among those you must invite are representatives of any group that may be affected. Bringing such persons into the process right from the start will get their viewpoints, concerns, and talents into the mix from the get-go. They have a lot to offer—don't make the common mistake of ignoring them. Worse, don't assume that "we" know best, and that "we" will do something for "them." "Them" folks just happen to have a particular need; we all have our particular needs. "Them" folks just happen to have resources too—many resources of which we would be totally unaware until we talked and worked with them. We must learn to share both our needs and our resources. That's the participatory way to go about this.

Before we go any further, however, let's get out of the way some common mistakes that very well-meaning people make as they undertake a project for good. We're going to review a bit here and raise some new issues as well.

Choosing a Goal, Not a Resource nor an Activity

Remember our discussion of resources, activities, and results. A simple example will, I believe, suffice to remind us of the relationship between these concepts:

(handwritten note in left margin:) What do you want to accomplish? How is a different (resource) question.

Cash Grant	➡	School	➡	Educated Children
Resource	➡	Activity	➡	Result
		Or		
Input	➡	Output	➡	Outcome/Impact/Goal

We know that most people donate money as their way of investing in change for good. Individuals make contributions to philanthropic causes; groups make grants to local charities. And that's good. Where it turns out to be unfortunate, however, is when people mistake the resource, the money, for the goal. Ideally, the resource should be employed in some *activity* that we have decided will achieve the *result* we intend. We will have defined a problem and used the resource and the activity to attempt to solve it.

Here's an example of a group confusing their activity of awarding grants—of providing resources—with their goal, which was stated as rooting out the causes of poverty, homelessness, hunger, etc.

> ∾ A small, church-related disaster-response and development organization collected money during the year from members of its congregations across the country. At the same time, it accepted applications from small organizations, worldwide, seeking grants for specific projects.
>
> The board had set very broad guidelines, so virtually any project was eligible. Most of the board members had little experience in grant-making or program evaluation. Nevertheless, twice a year, the board of directors would review the applications and choose those to fund.
>
> At the end of the board meeting, the board would add up the amount of money it had granted to be sure it had in hand the necessary funds. Subsequent press releases and annual reports

focused on the total amount of money given away and on the description of each funded project as it appeared in the grant application.

No mechanism was set up to monitor the use of funds during the program year. Nor was the board engaged in project-end evaluation. Grant recipients were asked to file a year-end report on the use of the grant money. In reality, few did. The grantees had no incentive to comply with this reporting requirement, since one of the board's policies was that no organization could receive a grant two years in a row. Grantees had no reason to provide a report, since they were ineligible for renewal grants anyhow. ∽

This is a clear example of mistaking resources for results. In fairness, some of the funded projects may well have accomplished some good somewhere. Others . . . who knows? But certainly there is a better way to do good, and to the board's credit, they soon recognized that. They chose to rethink their operations completely. They revised their policies, and chose only two areas that they would fund—food security and primary health. Most important, they got out of the business of responding to over-the-transom grant applications and instead hired professional staff to initiate responsible programming.

A second example reminds us of the confusion between activity and result.

∽ *A well-intentioned group of individuals on safari in Africa discovered, to their dismay, that the little girls in a certain village were not going to school. In discussions among themselves on the plane ride back to the U.S., the group concocted a grand surprise for the village: They would build a new school, specifically for girls. What a bold idea, they thought, and one that would transform the lives of these little girls. So they returned home, got their friends and neighbors excited about this idea, raised the money, hired an African builder, built the school, and even raised enough money to pay a teacher.*

But the little girls still didn't go to school. Why? Because in that culture, little girls are responsible for obtaining the family's water supply. The nearest well was over two miles away, so the little girls trudged back and forth every day, carrying the water for the family's cooking and washing. In doing so, they walked right by the local elementary school but were too busy fetching water to go in.

The little girls didn't need a school. They needed a well. The problem was not the lack of school; the problem was the lack of water. ༄

If the group had focused on the desired result—educated girls—rather than the method—a school—they might have asked the right questions instead of presuming they knew the answer. They might have chosen the right answer instead of wasting their time and resources. Here is a perfect example, as well, of what happens when we neglect to involve the affected community in our decision-making process.

[handwritten margin note: Focus on the desired result rather than the method.]

[handwritten margin note: Involve the affected community in the decision-making.]

Choosing to Achieve, Not Do

So that brings us to our final point in this section. Through careful assessment and candid exploration, we can focus on what we want to achieve—on our results, our goal—leaving the question of how to *do* it to a discussion of *activities* and *methods*, not *results*. What we want to achieve should be our starting point. Do we want healthy babies? Supportive group homes for the mentally ill? Better nutrition for those in Zimbabwe?

Each of these laudable achievements might be accomplished in myriad ways. Let's say that we are working with a Zimbabwean community. Jointly we have decided that the most important goal we could accomplish together would be better nutrition through improved production of their vegetable fields. Here are some choices of methods or activities we might employ:

- More productive seeds to increase yield per acre
- Increasing soil fertility
- Irrigation
- Growing different crops with greater nutritional value
- Better tools
- Mechanized farming
- Land redistribution (in Zimbabwe this was an ill-conceived move on the part of the government that has had disastrous results)
- Training for farmers in up-to-date agricultural methods
- Establishment of a farmers' cooperative to buy supplies or to get better prices for surplus produce
- New methods of preserving the food as it ripens

Even this list of choices is undoubtedly not exhaustive. But it is enough to get started.

Let's say that by consulting with the local farmers and the local agricultural experts, we come to the conclusion that we can have the greatest results by focusing on improving soil fertility. That activity could be made possible by some combination of the following resources:

- Money to buy better fertilizer
- Cooperative purchasing of fertilizer in bulk to lower the cost
- Hand spreaders to apply the fertilizer evenly and easily
- Well-digging equipment to provide water for application of liquid fertilizer
- Tractors to plow the fertilizer into the ground
- Oxen to plow the ground in areas with no access to fuel (with the result of more fertilizer as well)

Goal – what do you want to achieve

Activities – what will it take to do it

Resources – what do we need to support the activities

You'll note that the process we have used in this illustration above starts with what we want to *achieve*. We then work "backward" to the needed activities and then to the resources we would need to support those activities. In other words, we start with the desired result, determine the various options for activities or methods that could contribute to that result, and then consider the variety of resources that might be employed.

In this case, appropriate resources would be money, tools, equipment, and knowledge. For sake of this exercise, let's say that we choose a cooperative buying program. We'll assist the farmers in organizing the cooperative, setting up policies and rules, and steering them to reliable sources for them to purchase fertilizer in bulk quantities.

You will notice that we have chosen *only one* desired result, then chosen *only one* activity to employ, and then chosen *only those resources* that directly advance that method. In practice, however, when we get to the question of resources, we often find that several resources working together will achieve the greatest results in the quickest time.

This process may look complicated and difficult at first. Trust me, it is not. Once you employ it a time or two, it will become second nature.

Choosing the Journalistic Way

This is another tool we often use to help us assess our way forward. Budding journalists are continually reminded of the Five "Ws": *Who? What? Why? Where? When?* These questions can be extremely useful in examining options for our philanthropic or outreach efforts. Choosing with whom to work, to do what, why, where, and when, breaks down the process into manageable steps. Answers to each of the Five Ws will enable us to devise programs that meet all the basic steps that we discussed in Chapter 2.

The secret is to keep asking the questions until we get to a satisfactory answer. Let's look at a possible scenario. The chairwoman of a small women's club outreach committee is speaking:

> *"Let's decide what to do with the money we raised at our bake sale. Suzie proposes we buy groceries for hungry people."*

> *"Who needs groceries?" [Who?]*

> *"The Smith and Brown families."*

> *"Why are they hungry?" [Why?]*

> *"Because they don't have jobs."*

> *"What keeps them from getting jobs?" [What?]*

> *"They don't have money to get training [Why?] for the kinds of jobs in our community." [Where?]*

> *"Ah, ha. You mean that if we paid for job training, they could get jobs and buy food?"*

> *"Yes, but they would still be hungry until then." [When?]*

> *"OK, so instead of just giving them enough money to buy food, or giving them food, we could pay their tuition and provide groceries for the time it takes them to get the necessary training, right?"*

> *"That makes great sense!"*

You see, hunger wasn't the real problem here. Training was. But without pursuing the Five Ws process, the committee wouldn't have arrived at the right answer. Delivering groceries to a hungry family would have seemed the right and charitable thing to do, but it wouldn't have made a long-term difference. And it would have been a case of "help"—we have more than enough money and food, so we'll give you some of ours. This is the "Lady Bountiful" attitude, and we never want to fall into that trap.

Let's look at each of the Five Ws in a bit more detail so that you'll be able to use them as you decide just who your program partners will be, what you hope to achieve, why you select a certain activity, where you want to work, when you expect to engage in this activity, and when you expect to reach your goal.

Who?, or the Importance of Partnership

Remember in Chapter 1 we spoke about how we never "help" people. To help is to do *to* or do *for* someone. Instead, we want to do *with* others. In Chapter 2 we talked about partnerships. We talked about the importance of partners. We talked about the importance of working *together* to achieve our aims.

Partnerships can be of two kinds: You or your group may choose a partner (an individual or a group) with resources you lack. You or your group may partner with someone or some group to carry out complementary activities toward the desired end. One partner may dream up a new approach to the problem, a second may provide the resources, another one the relevant activities. Or you may have multiple partners at every level.

In each case, however, the proposed "beneficiaries" of the activity must be considered full and vital partners from the outset. They must be part of the planning, the resourcing, and the implementation. They must be treated as equals and with great respect. They will be quick to pick up on any hint of condescension or disregard.

Their participation will have many advantages. First, they understand the problem far better than you do, as they live with it every day. They are aware of cultural or political issues that may dictate your choice of activities. They see potential pitfalls. They know the history of the problem. They know what attempts at solution have been made previously and why they failed. They have a much better idea of what will work and what won't. They recognize who in the community needs to be involved.

Development experts talk about involving all "stakeholders." By stakeholder, they mean anyone who has a legitimate interest in the problem. A stakeholder in a medical program could be the ill person, the affected family, the local medical personnel, those supporting the medical clinic, the surrounding community (remember stories of community opposition to methadone clinics?), the ill person's medical insurance carrier, possibly Medicare or Medicaid—even pharmaceutical companies who might donate necessary medications.

You'll remember that involving all those involved in planning or carrying out a program is called "Participatory Community" process, and it is a critical step in constructing an effective program. We may think we have all the answers, but we don't. Look back at the example we gave earlier of the well-meaning folks who wanted to build a school for girls in Africa. Had they taken time to develop a partnership with the parents in the village, they would have learned the real reason the girls were not in school and would have addressed the right problem. (Good heavens, they could have simply asked one of the little girls, "Why don't you go to school?") The cost to dig a well might have been significantly less than building a school. Not only would the well have allowed the school-aged girls to attend school, it would also have provided ample clean drinking water to the entire community—perhaps enough to irrigate some crops as well. In fact, the money for the school might have been enough to dig wells in several communities, expanding the benefits far beyond only a small number of young girls.

Or another school example, this one a school in Honduras:

> A U.S. church group visited a small village several miles from the nearest town. School-aged children had to walk to and from the town school; as a result, most of them did not attend school regularly.
>
> Aha, said the tourists. What this village needs is its own school. And we've got the money to provide it for them. They did not ask the villagers how the education system worked in Honduras. They did not ask the villagers what they would need to support a school in

their own village. They just asked the villagers if they would like a school in their own village. The villagers were excited and grateful. These wealthy Americans were going to make it possible for their children to attend school right there.

(Note here the different result each group expects. The Americans think the result is the building. The Hondurans think their children are getting an education.)

So the Americans returned home, raised money, gathered a group of volunteers to go to the village to build the school and a little house for the teacher and, in less than a year, presented to the villagers a tidy little adobe school and an adjacent small two-bedroom home. After the dedication ceremony and warm congratulations all around, the Americans returned home to show pictures of their work.

Two years later, one member of that group happened to revisit the village. The school was in disrepair. The house was uninhabited and being used as a storeroom for grain. No classes were being held. The children were still walking miles to school—if they went at all. ∾

The reason? In that Central American country, the village must hire and pay the teacher. The villagers did not have the money for a teacher. So they had no way to take advantage of this gift.

Had the Americans spent some time talking with the villagers and the local government education authorities (both of them "stakeholders"), they would have learned this fact. They would have realized that the desired result was education for the children, not a schoolhouse. They might have explored other ways to achieve their goal. They could have looked at alternative choices. They might have chosen to purchase a school bus and underwrite the salary of a driver. Perhaps they could have raised additional money to hire a teacher. Perhaps they could have given a village mother a scholarship to go to school to learn to be the teacher. Perhaps they could have asked a PTA group back home to find a retired Spanish-speaking teacher to lead the school in the interim.

In each of these cases, the concept of *partnership* would have prevented misunderstandings and dashed hopes. In each case, the partnership would have made better use of the resources. The partnership would have exposed the flaw in the original idea and come up with viable alternatives.

We always start a better way of doing good by including those directly affected by our work as partners. From there we have a whole gamut of potential partners to consider. Obviously, choosing the right ones is extremely important. The right partners can ensure we focus on the right result, undertake the key activities, and employ the right resources in the right amount. The right partners can make our work so much easier and more productive.

Consequently, choosing partners should be a deliberate and well-thought-out process. The right partner is a blessing. The wrong one can be a curse. Taking our time to find the right partner can be critical to our success. To rush headlong into a partnership can result in wasted resources and time, ill-will or hurt feelings, and even failure.

One common mistake many well-meaning groups make is to learn about a problem somewhere from an interested party, then immediately hook up with that person to form a "partnership" to address the problem. Here is an almost unbelievable, but true story.

> ∽ *A Southeast Asian woman (but she could have been from anywhere) was in the United States for medical treatment (or so she said). She attended a Sunday worship service at a wealthy suburban church and engaged some of the congregation in conversation. She described in vivid detail the dire need for primary education in her home village and enthralled them with her dream to build a school. She had the land, she said, left to her by her late father. She had attended teacher's college, she said, and was certified to teach in her home land.*
>
> *Her listeners were so captivated by her imagination, her energy, and her enthusiasm, not to mention her "exoticness," that they convinced the church to take up a collection right then and there for the woman's project.*
>
> *Before meeting this woman, the members of the church had never thought of supporting an education project in Asia. They knew nothing about the sector (education) or the region (Asia). Even after hearing the woman's plans, they did no research. They didn't bring in education experts to talk with the woman about her plans. They didn't search out people with knowledge of the woman's country,*

and village, to verify her authenticity. They didn't explore whether primary education was actually available or not in the village.

The clue that something was amiss was right there, right in front of them. The woman, claiming difficulty in transferring bank funds to her country, asked that the church's donations be given to her in cash. That should have given the congregation pause.

The request for the money in cash should have been a huge warning flag, and several people were suspicious, but no one wanted to be the proverbial "wet blanket" or be accused of not being compassionate. So no one spoke up.

The members of the congregation were so transfixed by the thought that they could make a difference somewhere at very little cost and no effort that they wound up victims of a scam. They never heard from the woman again. "Look what we can do for them" rapidly turned into "Look what she has done to us." ∽

The lesson here is the same lesson we've talked about over and over: We must start by choosing the *result* we want to achieve. We can then look for the right partners. If we want a well-educated populace in a rural town in Nebraska, we should partner with the school system—administrators, teachers, student leaders, curriculum counselors—the taxing authorities, the parent-teacher organization, and town board of education. If we want to support the international movement to "Make Poverty History," we will want choose partners who understand the causes and ramifications of poverty, know what interventions are most effective, and are efficient at implementing them.

If we want to increase civic pride in our town, we might undertake a partnership with the local garden club to plant flowers in public places and with the local Boy Scouts to pick up trash from the roadsides. (Be careful and think through all implications whenever you join in a project by working with others. A local Kiwanis Club had partnered with the local Boy Scout troop for just such a roadside clean-up for several years before they discovered that the boys were not covered by the Club's insurance policies. They quickly remedied the situation, to the relief of all.)

Knowing what we want to achieve will enable us to narrow the selection of possible partners.

[margin note: Choose the result then partners if needed]

Remember, though, that we must always include as partners those who will benefit from our activities. If the villagers in Honduras or Africa or Asia would have been brought into partnership to eliminate the barriers to education in their villages, donors would quickly have learned that their initial impulse wouldn't solve the problems at all. If the church members had just checked out the story of the woman wanting to build the school, they would have been spared the embarrassment of being victims of a scam.

We know that working in partnership sometimes takes longer than going it alone. Sometimes working in partnership is frustrating. Sometimes the partnership breaks down. But in almost every case, if the anticipated result is going to be achieved by using the available resources most effectively and efficiently, then choosing to work in partnership is the only way to go.

Remember, all parties to solving a problem have resources—some are much more apparent than others. The villagers in Honduras or Africa might not have had money or tools, but they had information. Undoubtedly they were well aware of their problems and had their own ideas about appropriate solutions. They may well have had time, and skills, and creativity to dedicate to a solution. They were willing to work at the solution. We risk missing out on these resources by not engaging in partnership.

So the question of choosing *Who?* is simple. We work with whoever has a piece of the puzzle, has resources to offer, has desire to be part of the solution. We think in terms of partnership, of doing together, not in terms of "doing for others."

One other way of looking at the *Who?* that we must consider is this: Who else is doing this program or one like it? By identifying *Who else?* we will find those who are already engaged in solving the problem (and with whom we might partner), those who have tried to solve it and failed (we can learn a lot from them), and those who have undertaken similar projects or worked in the same geographic area (we can learn a lot from them as well). So don't ask just *Who?* Be sure to also ask *Who else?*

Now turn to Exercise 3-2 and refresh your thinking about the *Who?* questions.

Choosing *Who?*

For all the following exercises, 3-2 through 3-4, we are going to assume that you have uncovered a serious problem in your community that could be solved by the building of a free-standing teen center (never mind right now what that particular problem is—you don't need to know that to do the following exercises).

Who?

Your first task is to make a list of all those who should be involved in planning and building this teen center. If you take a few minutes, I suspect that you can come up with at least twenty people or groups of people.

_____   _____

_____   _____

_____   _____

_____   _____

_____   _____

_____   _____

_____   _____

_____   _____

_____   _____

_____   _____

Why?, or the Importance of Motive

Why? has two components: Why the *problem?* and Why are *we* the ones who want to tackle it? Each *Why?* is important, and neither can be neglected. Let's start in the reverse order with our own motive. Let's start by understanding our own motives for undertaking an assistance program. Knowing exactly why we want to work in some particular sector (health, education, housing) or geographic area, instead of some other sector or area, is often overlooked in our enthusiasm to get on with the work. But careful self-examination may prevent our choosing the wrong kind of activity, at the wrong time, for the wrong purpose, possibly making things even worse than they were before.

In answer to the question *Why?* let's look at some possible motivations we might hear:

> *My tax accountant says I've got to increase my charitable giving this year.*
>
> *My neighbor is involved in this youth tutoring program and wants me to participate, too.*
>
> *We are the church "Outreach Committee." We make grants each year.*
>
> *We met this medical student from Kenya, and he wants us to raise money to build a clinic in his village.*
>
> *We love the band U2. Since they want to "Make Poverty History," so do we.*

You now have learned enough to spot the missing *Why?* here. Why do I have the money, and why do I have to give it away? Why should I participate in my neighbor's program? Why should my church give grants, and to whom, for what? Why follow the lead of a rock band?

Understanding our own motives, our group's motive, and the motives of all the partners we plan to bring into the project will clear the air for all concerned. If we know why we want to do something, we'll know what we, personally, want to get out of it, and we'll be more likely to be satisfied.

Conversely, if we are not clear about our motive, we may well be dissatisfied. Let's say we choose to engage in an outreach program because we want to get to know the social leaders in our community who are active in it. But if those leaders operate virtually as a closed clique, not opening their small circle to new people, we are likely to be severely frustrated in our participation in the program, as valuable as it may be.

So are motives like that bad motives? Well, certainly there are wrong motives for particular situations. But no motive is a *bad* motive so long as it is legal, moral, and ethical. The motive might be inappropriate, or expensive, or contradictory, but it still might not be a *bad* motive. It might be just the wrong motive at the right time.

Even if we don't meet and get to know the local "society," we will still achieve some good by participating in the outreach program. We may be disappointed, but that doesn't mean that we haven't done something worthwhile.

Much good has been done in the world for what we might consider the "wrong" motive. Major scientific breakthroughs have occurred when the scientist was engrossed in pursuit of some totally different objective. After all, Columbus landed in the New World when his motive was finding a new route to the Far East.

What is regrettable is our not recognizing our own motive when we become involved in a program and then being unhappy with the result. So it behooves us to be brutally honest with ourselves and acknowledge our own motives for engaging in a program to do good.

Engaging in the second kind of *Why?* can actually be rather fun. This is how we narrow our choices as we investigate whatever program we want to pursue. In this case, we repeatedly respond to whatever is proposed by asking "Why?" We keep asking this over and over until we get to a clear answer—the so-called "root cause." We ask "Why?" until we find a program that actually produces the desired result. We don't want to use our resources willy-nilly; we don't want to spin our wheels carrying out ineffective activities. We want to tackle and solve a problem. So we ask why and why and why until we get to the crux of the problem. That will clarify our choices.

Ask why to clarify choices

I think you get the point. Let's take one example. Pay particular attention to resources, activities, and results.

> *"I propose we donate money [resource] for a teen center [activity]."*
>
> *"Why build a teen center?"*
>
> *"Because we need to educate our teens about the dangers of using drugs [desired result]."*
>
> *"Why would their own place [activity] provide that education about drugs [result]?"*
>
> *"Well, maybe it wouldn't, but a teen center is a good idea [activity]."*
>
> *"Why?"*
>
> *"Well, they need some place to go [activity]."*
>
> *"Why?*
>
> *"Because the school doesn't offer an after-school program [activity]."*
>
> *"Why?"*
>
> *"They say they have the room but not the money [resource]."*
>
> *"So maybe we should fund [resource] an afterschool program [activity] at the school instead of building a teen center?"*
>
> *"That would be a great idea."*
>
> *"But why would that solve the drug problem [desired result]?"*
>
> *"Oh, I see your point. Maybe we need to think of something other than a teen center. Maybe we need a teen mentoring program [activity]."*

And the *Why?* process starts all over.

Continuing to ask why, with a clear understanding of the difference between resource and activity, will eventually bring us to the most effective program.

The goal here is to choose among the many possible solutions to the problem. Often, only a clear understanding of the problem will enable us to construct the correct response. So we need to keep asking why until we are sure that we have defined the problem, investigated alternative programs to fix it, and have the resources to carry out the necessary activities. The resources and the activity are important, but only the result truly matters.

Where to Work

Where do you want to work? Very often that choice is dictated to you by policies of your organization. The policies of church groups, civic associations, and social organizations often require that all outreach activities be undertaken to benefit residents of the local area. Conversely, some organizations and private foundations are formed specifically to address international causes, such as the Millennium Development Goals.

A common mistake made by organizations is believing that they need to be part of a big international program in order to be useful. But even those organizations with a focus strictly on their own communities can have great impact.

An initiative called Open Table is collaboration in the truest sense. A coalition of about a dozen people brings one person or a family from "poverty to wholeness" in a structured program over eight months. Each Open Table coalition includes an array of volunteer professionals from finance, medicine, counseling, and other services. Every one of those engaged in the program is rewarded. Coalition members rejoice when they see someone moving from dependency to true self-sufficiency. The lives of the person or family assisted are forever transformed. They become role models for others who seek out Open Table programs for themselves. This is a program easily replicated at very low cost with just the skills available in almost any group—including church congregations.

If you are reading this book as an individual rather than being part of a group, you may have more latitude in choosing the scope of your activities. You probably have far more freedom in choosing the problem you'd like to solve. You can work on a small but important problem in your own community, drawing on familiar and local resources and partnering with friends and neighbors. You also have the choice to join others in an existing joint effort to tackle a broader problem. Perhaps you want to tackle a national problem, bringing your own ideas, creativity, and talents to work in concert with those of your partners. Or you can venture farther afield, starting or supporting an international venture.

The fact that you are only one person should not deter you. If you clearly see a problem and have the ability to find ways to solve it, go at it. Undertake a bold program, consult with necessary partners, and achieve your goal. Anthropologist Margaret Mead once said, "Never doubt that a small group of thoughtful, committed citizens can change the world. Indeed, it is the only thing that ever has."

Depending upon where you chose to work, you will reap particular benefits and encounter specific drawbacks. Let's sketch them:

Working Locally

Working locally is sometimes both easier and more difficult.

Benefits: Working locally, you are more likely to know whom to consult, what options and resources are available to you, who might be opposed to the program and why. You understand the local politics and culture. You probably have a circle of friends who can be brought into the project or, at least, will give you moral support. You can have "hands-on" involvement every step of the way. You have the power to create the solution, or negotiate away the problem.

Drawbacks: You will likely encounter opposition from those invested in maintaining the current situation. You will undoubtedly hear, "But we've always done it this way." If the situation has existed for some time, apathy will be a big hurdle. You will have a harder time creating excitement about the program among those with resources or influence.

When we do not have a choice in where we will work (perhaps because of our organization's policies or donor preferences), we need to be certain that the problem is solvable at the imposed level. If we can work only in a small geographic area, we may not be able to tackle a more widespread systemic problem. If we are concerned about high unemployment in our town, but we live in the Rust Belt, we may need to consider advocacy efforts in collaboration with other involved citizens. We may not be able, on our own, to create jobs in our town without considering the situation throughout the region. In that case, we might need to join a coalition of other local groups in order to address the larger issue.

Working at a Distance

Working in a distant locale (whether in your own country or abroad) has its own benefits and its own drawbacks.

Benefits: You can capitalize on the excitement and enthusiasm of learning about and working in a new, and perhaps "exotic," environment. You can exercise your creativity to tackle a problem that doesn't exist at home (lack of potable water, for example). You will make new friends. You will learn about a different culture. Your dollars may go a lot farther because of differences in the cost of living, cultural norms, or even climate. (Houses in Central America are less expensive to build because labor costs are less, and the houses do not need to be winter-tight.)

Drawbacks: You will be unfamiliar with local customs, political processes, and laws. You may have to work with people who speak a different language, creating the very real possibility of misunderstandings. You will undoubtedly encounter unrealistic expectations (on all sides) due to existing stereotypes ("rich Americans," for example, or "lazy natives").

Neither these benefits nor these drawbacks should dictate where you choose to work. They are important—even critical to eventual success—but they are not defining. You simply need to be aware of them, to name them. With a bit of effort, you can choose ways to enhance the benefits and minimize or even eliminate the drawbacks.

Also remember that the world is becoming a smaller place. Conditions in one part of the world often affect people in distant lands. International trade agreements may open new markets for small farmers. Or they may make imported food so inexpensive that the small farmers can't make a living. Conversely, tariffs or subsidies may prevent the free flow of goods. Inexpensive sea transport and low wages make clothing from China so cheap that domestic apparel factories shut down, eliminating thousands of jobs. Movies give people in distant lands a skewed vision of the wealth in America or Europe.

Today's rapid worldwide communications are both exciting and frightening. We know what is happening at any moment almost anywhere in the world. We see how people live and work. We can transmit information effortlessly. Cell phones have made remote villages as close as our next door neighbor. Tom Friedman, in his book *The World is Flat*, celebrates this global connectivity as a "newfound power for *individuals* to collaborate . . . globally. [This] is enabling, empowering, and enjoining individuals and small groups to go global so easily and seamlessly."

At the same time, with all this interconnectivity, we are brought into close contact with so many of the ills in this world. We see people struggling with challenges we have long overcome. We conquered malaria in Philadelphia and Washington, D.C., more than a century ago. We ensured free primary and secondary education for our children. We raise enough grain to feed the world (even though we do have hungry people here at home). We are aware more than ever before of the great disparity between those in the so-called developed world and those who have yet to benefit from technological advances.

So we are presented with the opportunity to work farther and farther from home. At the same time we see unmet needs right around the corner.

Where you choose to work will have major influences on what you do, with whom you partner, and how you go about implementing your program. Those whose geographic area is determined for them—a community foundation, for example—will be spared the initial decision of where, but will have to navigate the local situations and advocates. Those whose geographic area is not pre-determined have more options, making it harder to decide.

What Is the Problem and *What* Can We Do?

OK. We now understand the need to assess carefully the *Who?*, the *Why?*, and the *Where?*. Only two issues remain: *What?* and *When?* We're getting there, aren't we? Yep, so stick with me here for a bit longer.

The component that we are calling the *What?* can be easily misunderstood. We need to be really, really clear about this. We are not talking here about what we are going to do. That is part of the resources/activities/results discussion. We are not talking about what program to implement, or what resources we'll need, or even what result we hope to achieve, per se.

No, when we talk about *What?*, we mean: <u>*What's the problem?*</u>

Beware of quick answers to that question. Remember Pogo. Remember "We have met the enemy, and he is us." Jumping to conclusions about the exact cause of a situation makes us the enemy to the right solution. The real problem may not be apparent at first or even second or third glance. What appears to be the problem may in fact be only a result of the true situation. Remember our device of continuing to ask *Why?* That process, if carried to its conclusion, will improve our chances to arrive at the right *What?*

So refrain from jumping to conclusions. Take the time to explore, to ask the necessary questions. You have already learned many of the necessary techniques. Much of the previous discussions unavoidably touched on discerning the problem. The techniques we have already learned in the *Who?*, *Why?*, *Where?* sections are excellent tools to employ.

The *Why?* discussion gave us a useful method ("Keep asking *Why?*") to arrive at a sensible answer.

The *Who?* discussion encouraged us to involve all the stakeholders, pointing out their valuable capacity to bring new and different perspectives and information. By seeking out all potential partners, we identify those who have a vested interest in this problem and in its solution.

Tackling *Where?*, we explored possible program locales and touched on benefits and pitfalls inherent in various options. Working locally is dramatically different from working abroad. When we have a choice, we need to be aware of all these differences. We need to recognize the need for special expertise, unique approaches, particular resources.

Exercise 3-3 will help you think about where you might want to work.

Choosing *Where*

Think of your own community. Imagine that you are part of a group—a church mission outreach committee, or a men's civic organization, or a county medical association, or a young women's social service organization, or some other group to which you belong. Imagine that you have been given the task of proposing four potential sites, two in the United States and two abroad, for a teen center outreach program. List them below and list at least one advantage and one disadvantage for working in that area (find a different advantage and disadvantage for each one!).

- _____

_____

_____

- _____

_____

_____

- _____

_____

_____

- _____

_____

_____

By employing the techniques of *Who?*, *Why?*, *Where?*, and *When?*, we inch closer to identifying the problem we are going to choose to address—the *What?*

Stop right here for a minute. This is an appropriate place for a reality check. Keep in mind that old bugaboo, the danger of unintended consequences. What are undoubtedly good works in one area may have adverse impact elsewhere. Solving one problem can exacerbate other plights. Solving one problem may simply create another, and perhaps more serious, problem.

For example, reducing child mortality in developing countries creates a need for more food for more children. Making higher education readily available leaves graduates frustrated if they can't find appropriate jobs (the situation right now in some of the oil-rich countries in the Middle East).

On a social policy level, think of these two examples: Smokey the Bear's campaign to prevent forest fires has led to overgrowth and a buildup of dead wood that increases the severity and size of naturally occurring fires. Building dams and dikes on the rivers of the Midwest has increased the number of major floods.

Certainly, not all unintended consequences are bad. If your program produces wonderful unforeseen consequences, that's great. But better than being surprised, we should try to anticipate all consequences of our action and be prepared to deal with them, good or bad.

Now that we've reminded ourselves of the danger of unintended consequences, we come to the fun part. At least I've always thought this section was the most energizing part of this whole process.

We're going to investigate the second part of *What?*: What can we do?

Remember, we've already addressed the first *What?*: What's the problem? And we think we've narrowed the problem down to its most basic part or parts. We are comfortable with our conclusion. We can state the problem in simple terms and are convinced that we teased out the causes and avoided easy answers. We are ready to look at the second *What?*: What can we do?

[handwritten margin notes: What's the problem? What can we do?]

Note the tense of that verb. Not what *shall* we do, not what *should* we do, but what *can* we do. There's a big difference.

Deciding (the topic of the next chapter) is not the same as investigating. Deciding which one of the viable alternatives we *shall* do will happen only after we dedicate all our creativity, our ingenuity, our imagination to the cataloguing, to the choosing of what we *can* do. We need to explore every possible solution, sensible or not. We need to look down every path to see where it will lead us. We need to research similar programs for hints. Maybe something didn't work for others, but would work just fine for us. We need to do some of what I call "embroidering"—taking a blank piece of cloth and adding layer and layer of color and design to it until a pattern appears.

Cataloging what we *can* do—what we *could* do—is a perfect place for brainstorming—you know, where a group of people throw out any and all ideas and are prohibited from criticizing anyone's input during the session.

What you want is a huge list of possible interventions. Some will be silly, some impractical, some old-hat. Some will appear to be brilliant. Others will probably be weird. But nestled in that list will be the seeds of your program.

Notice that I said seeds, not seed. Right now we aren't finalizing our decision. What we want now are two or three (or even more) possible choices we could make. Take your time. Take a deep breath. Think it over. Mull it over. Talk it over.

Also remember Murphy's Law: If anything can go wrong, it will. Therefore a useful tool to apply in the *What?* analysis is to ask yourself how many ways each possible path could go wrong?

- Whom might it hurt?
- How might it create additional hardships?
- Who might have the power/influence to derail your activities?
- What vital resources might be missing?
- How sure are you of the commitment/abilities of your partners?
- Whom have you left out?
- And, of course, what could be the unintended consequences?

You can probably add to this list of questions. The more questions you ask (and answer), the greater likelihood that you will develop an inventory of possibly effective programs.

You will want to come up with an exhaustive list of activities that meet all your requirements: they are achievable, are practical, are efficient, and are effective uses of available resources. You must have agreement on these activities from all the major stakeholders—or know the reason why a certain stakeholder does not agree with you. This list of choices is starting to point you in the direction of your final decision.

When to Start and How Long Will it Take?

The simple answer to the first part is: start when you are ready. And the second question: it'll take as long as it takes!

But let's get beyond simple answers—although, in truth, the simple answer is pretty dead-on.

When should we start? We should <u>start when we have enough information to make us confident that we have uncovered the root cause</u> of the problem, we understand why it exists, we've chosen the right place to work and identified our partners. We have also explored different ways that we might address the problem. Be careful. We haven't yet decided what we will *do*. We're still concentrating at this time on what problem we're going to tackle and looking at what different programs might fix it. Choosing which of those alternatives comes later, in the next chapter, "Decision."

Sooner or later, and usually sooner, someone is going to ask: How long will this take? At this point, you can't honestly answer. We gave one flippant answer above: As long as it takes. More realistically, however, <u>the rule of thumb is that it will take twice as long as you think.</u> Another smart-aleck answer, I know, but one that is probably more accurate than you want to believe.

Impatience is our biggest worry here. In this regard, we resemble first-time gardeners. We choose what vegetable we want to eat (the problem), decide to grow the vegetables (the activity), find a place for a garden plot (decide where we want to work), choose the seeds at the garden center (the resources), and plant them. If they don't sprout quickly enough for us, we conclude that we must have done something wrong and start all over. Had we been patient just a few more days, we might have been rewarded with a bumper crop of delicate little seedlings.

So it is with outreach. We have to have patience. We will plant our seeds and tend our garden, but we can't expect results overnight. Just as the gardener has to contend with insect pests, flooding rainstorms, wind damage, or drought, so we will have to contend with conditions beyond our control that will affect our timing and our results.

(Note that in the example above, we could have obtained the desired veggie by going to the supermarket, or the local farmers' market. Growing it ourselves wasn't our only choice.)

Not that we shouldn't consider time constraints. We all know that attention spans are limited. We start out with great enthusiasm and energy, but as time wears on, we wear down. As projects drag out, we begin to lose interest. That's just human nature, and we must take this fact into account.

Biting off more than we can chew usually refers to the size of the mouthful. But here it doesn't apply just to the size of the project. It also refers to the time frame of the problem. It cautions us against embarking on a project of longer-term duration than we can sustain. Ongoing organizations whose focus is on outreach naturally have a longer time horizon than ad hoc groups of well-intentioned individuals whose sole purpose for banding together is to address a particular issue.

Therefore, rather than asking how much time something will *take*, we should ask ourselves how much time we have to *give*. Can we keep going until we reach our goal? Can we prolong our interest? Can we carry on when we hit the inevitable snags? When the project drags on and on? When some of us drop out, leaving the rest of us carrying the full load?

Turn now to the final exercise in this chapter, Exercise 3-4, and think about the "whens" that could affect your work.

Choosing *When?*

Your final exercise in this chapter is to pick one of the locations that you have chosen for your teen center, and then to list any event that might affect when you could start the project, or what might delay (or speed up) the process.

- _____

  _____

  _____

  _____

  _____

  _____

  _____

  _____

  _____

  _____

  _____

  _____

Once you have completed these exercises you might understandably be ready to throw in the towel. Who would have thought there were so many things to consider? How in the world can I work through all these choices? Do I really have to?

I can hear your thoughts right now: "Golly, I just wanted to do something good, and you're telling me I have to do all this stuff first?"

Well, yes, you do, if you want to achieve your goal at the least cost in time and resources. This process is the better way of doing good. Going through all these steps will load the dice in your favor. It will raise the chances that your program will be effective. And you certainly want to make best use of all the resources you have at hand so you have the best outcome.

However, I recognize that the *When?* question brings up those situations that demand our immediate attention. Some things have to be done *right away*. Some problems demand that the answer to "When?" is "Now."

Sometimes the need is so overwhelming we don't have the luxury of going through all these steps. Responding to a natural disaster, such as a tornado or a hurricane, requires prompt action. An outbreak of a virulent disease such as SARS or Ebola hemorrhagic fever would certainly call for immediate action, if only to prevent its spread.

In those "we-have-do-something-*now*" cases, we would be wise to remember the very practical words of Theodore Roosevelt: "Have you got a problem? Do what you can where you are with what you've got."

Otherwise, work through the process. You'll be glad you did.

Summary

Choosing what we might do to solve a problem is a multi-step process. If we follow some simple steps, we will be able to find several alternatives that might meet our needs. We need to think about what choices we have regarding our particular role—*investor, intermediary, implementer, or innovator*. We need to think about our choice of potential partners. We need to consider the five Journalistic Questions: *Who?, Why?, Where?, When?,* and *What?*

Finally, we have to recognize that emergency situations will trump all this planning. In those cases, we must forego our planning in order to act quickly in order to save lives.

Decision

Almost every problem we could think of could possibly be solved in several different ways. Choosing which one to undertake depends upon our available resources, our time, and our abilities.

In this chapter you will learn several mechanisms to narrow your choices so that you finally come to the best decision. You will learn how to judge the usefulness of available resources. You will learn the importance of budgets, cash-flow analyses, and timelines. You will use these tools to explore alternative paths to your goal and choose the one best suited to you or your group. You will make your decision.

And once you have decided upon the best route, you'll want to prepare and sign a memorandum of understanding with each of your program partners.

The time has come. You gotta decide.

Or should it be: Finally, you *get* to decide?

I can hear you now. "Good," you are sighing. "We've finally gotten to the point." You've been patient. You've worked through all the exercises. You've explored all the basic stuff—the definitions, the rationales, the whole process—and now you're ready.

You are now ready to select the problem that lies within your power to correct. You have thought carefully about what social ill you want to address. You know you must find all possible partners and consult with them, including those that the problem most affects. At the same time, you have focused on the problem, not on the people. You know you have to state your goal in terms of fixing something, not "helping" someone.

At this point in this new and better process, you will need to prepare six key documents. These documents will guide you as you choose exactly which program will best get you to your goal, to solving your problem. The same documents will guide you as you undertake your planned activities. They will help you monitor your progress, and evaluate your program. They will tell you what resources you need, and when you'll need them. They will ensure that you and your partners are all on the same page regarding mutual responsibilities throughout your progress. And yes, these documents must be in writing.

Remember that old saying, the job is not finished until the paperwork is done? Oh, I know it was the caption to an amusing cartoon, but maybe if you remember the cartoon, you'll remember this important point. No matter whether you are just one person, undertaking an exciting venture that you're eager to start, or whether you are a member of a group deliberating carefully on a future course of action, you must deal with the paperwork.

Not that the paperwork is difficult or is going to take a great deal of time. In fact, properly set up, the right paperwork can actually save your time (and effort and even money). If you spend the time to prepare in writing just six key documents, you will have greased the wheels and gunned the motor. Not getting things in writing can bog your journey down in mud or even slide you off the road. At the very least, you'll certainly waste gas. So let's turn the key, start the motor, and get going.

DOCUMENT NO. 1
The Goal

Let's review what you learned in Chapter 3 about goals. This might seem to be a bit repetitious, but I can't stress enough: Getting your goal summarized in one succinct, *written* sentence is probably the most important document you will have. Your goal is your guiding star. It is your destination. It is your hope, your dream, your target. This is where you are going. Remember, if you don't have a destination in mind, any road will take you there. And you'll probably wind up at a dead end.

To refresh our memory of how a goal should be expressed, here are some examples:

> *We will ensure that our middle-school students know the dangers of experimenting with marijuana.*
>
> *We will reduce the death rate among newborns in Nepal.*
>
> *We will ensure that every immigrant in our community has a chance to learn English.*
>
> *We will enrich the daily lives of those in our low-income senior housing.*
>
> *We will improve the health of those in a small community in Rwanda by reducing the incidence of water-borne diseases.*

Note the tense of the verb in each of these goals. We *will*. Not that we want to, or hope to, or try to. We *will*. This attitude of "we will" is crucial. It can make the difference between a successful project and an unsuccessful attempt.

I'm not being picky here. This is not just semantic nuance or grammar-school teacher fuddy-duddyism—how we phrase something actually sends a very clear message to all those involved.

When we say "we will," we demonstrate confidence, knowledge, and determination. We convey the assurance that the program will succeed. People will have faith in our approach and will want to join with us.

Moreover, choosing the right word to describe your solution will change how you yourself look at that solution. And saying that "we will" is a whole lot better than saying "we want" (to do something).

The same way with our goal. The difference between "We *want to reduce* the death rate among newborns in Nepal" and "We *will reduce* the death rate . . ." is enormous. *Wanting* is not *doing*. We can *want* all we want—but that doesn't accomplish anything. We have to believe that what we expect to happen is achievable. We have to invest the necessary talents to make it happen.

We know we can't just "want" to get a good grade in college—we have to study for it. We know we can't just "want" a good golf swing—we have to practice and practice. We know we can't just "want" our business to be profitable—we have to invest time and skill and energy and creativity into making it so. We also have to believe—to believe that if we study, or practice, or work hard, we will achieve our goal.

So it is in development—in charity or outreach or philanthropy, whatever you choose to call your work. If we are going to do something, if we are actually going to solve the problem, then we need to start out believing that we will do so—that we will, in fact, through our efforts, reduce the death rate among newborns in Nepal. We need to be sure that we are stating our goal precisely, so that everyone will understand what we plan to achieve.

You might be tempted to call your goal your "mission," or "mission statement." Resist that temptation. Most organizations already have a mission statement (or should). That is not the same as the goal of a particular program.

"Mission" usually means a hoped-for utopian situation. The World Bank has a wonderful mission statement: *Our dream is a world free of poverty*. Will they ever achieve their mission? Probably not, but the World Bank uses that mission statement to guide all their programs. And those programs each have an articulated goal. Each program's goal is an achievable target that, together with all the other program goals, will enable the World Bank to progress toward fulfilling its mission.

Furthermore, the term "mission" or "mission statement" frequently carries nuances beyond what we are considering here. Those hearing of the "mission" of a secular organization often confuse it with the work of religious "missionaries"—an unintentional but misleading interpretation. The whole term "mission" is somewhat vague and ethereal (and probably should be).

What we want with our goal statement is a very straight-forward, feet-on-the-ground sentence. We want our goal to be important, realistic, and achievable by us with the resources available to us. And in the time frame we have established.

To reinforce our understanding, let's now write down our goal.

_____

_____

_____

_____

Now look at your goal statement: Are you happy with it? Is it worded as a solution, rather than a band-aid? Is it succinct—one sentence?

Does it say *exactly* what you want to accomplish? Does it tell what you *will* do instead of what you *want* to do? Does it say what your end product is going to look like?

If so, fantastic. Celebrate this step. Congratulate yourself. Of all the activities that go into good outreach, knowing what you will accomplish is the first and most important. Now that you have clearly stated your goal, you can add the other key factors in your program's final decision.

 If you have any doubts, however, go to Exercise 4-1 and walk through writing your goal. The steps there will help you think through your project and express exactly what you intend to do. This goal-setting is probably the most important exercise in this entire chapter, so we want to be sure we're all on board.

Goal Setting

In the space below, describe the goal of your proposed program.

_____

_____

_____

_____

_____

_____

Now see if you can reduce that goal to 25 words or fewer.

_____

_____

_____

_____

Now check your goal against the requirements listed above :

    Does it say exactly what you want to accomplish?

    Does it tell what you _will_ do instead of what you _want_ to do?

    Does it describe what your end product is going to look like?

If not, see if you can rephrase it to meet these criteria.

_____

_____

_____

DOCUMENT NO. 2
Resources

Very often, the resources that we have available will dictate our response to the goal—the activity we will undertake. If your group has access to lots and lots of volunteers but very little money, your options will be restricted to programs that rely mostly on volunteer help. If you are a wealthy individual wanting to give money to support research into the cause of a certain disease, you have many options: university laboratories, private research institutions, national organizations dedicated to eradicating that disease, advocacy programs.

Knowing what resources you have may limit your choices—tell you what you cannot do. But you should never let your resources dictate your path—tell you what you should do. Let's look at an example.

Assume that you are that wealthy philanthropist we talked about above. Before writing a check for some lab somewhere, you would want to research carefully what other universities and other laboratories are doing in this fight. Perhaps you should give your money to one of them. But maybe instead of underwriting a lab, a better way would be to spend your money advocating for greater government support of research. Maybe you should start a nationwide awareness campaign that could leverage your funds into much more money for research. Even if you have only money as your resource, you have lots of options as to how you spend it to achieve your goal.

Remember that possible partners are also resources—wonderful resources that can be of immense assistance to us. Remember particularly that the expected beneficiaries of your work are important partners at every step of the way.

You catalogued your available resources in Chapter 2. Go back and review what you have available. Refresh your mind as to the variety, kind, and amount of resources that you might be able to call upon. See if you can now add any other resources that have turned up since you completed the exercise—or ones that just now occurred to you.

Keep your list of resources handy. They will play a major role as you prepare the next document.

The Planned Activities that Lead to the Goal

OK, we've picked our goal and listed our resources. But we don't yet know exactly which resources (including which partners) we could best use to reach that goal. We are still considering several alternative programs, each of which might enable us to meet our goal. Depending upon our resources and our partners, we might have three or four ways we could go ahead. So the next step is to select some possible ways forward to see which one makes best use of our resources. That's where we are.

Just what do we mean by options, you ask? Well, to help you get started, for just a moment, let's go back to that goal of ensuring that our middle-school youngsters know the dangers of sampling marijuana. Let's look at some options, some activities, that might work for us.

Option No. 1: We could lock them up at home except when they were at school. That would probably prevent their dabbling in pot. (Wow, would that option create unintended consequences—and legal issues as well.)

Option No. 2: We could start a D.A.R.E. (Drug Abuse Resistance Education) chapter at school, assuming that one doesn't already exist.

Option No. 3: We could try to make it "cool" to abstain by getting popular school jocks to endorse an "Only Wimps Try Pot" campaign.

Option No. 4: We could advocate for tougher laws for pushers.

Option No. 5: We could hold information sessions for parents, giving them tools and rationales to convince their teenagers.

I'm sure you can come up with five or ten other possible optional programs that might result in our goal of letting our teens know the dangers of trying marijuana. Some of these options would reinforce each other—we might want to take on two or even three of them simultaneously. Some of these options require considerable resources; we would need to be sure we can get them. Other options call upon the participation of several partners; we would need their complete buy-in. We want to be sure that we have both the resources and the energy to finish whatever we undertake.

For *each* option, or alternative, you will want to list all the activities you (or one of your partners) would need to undertake to achieve the goal. Sometimes you may need only one activity. Usually you will need several. Often you will need many, many activities, some necessarily preceding others.

Let's assume we have chosen to look more carefully at Option No. 2.

We want to list each step or activity that would be needed to accomplish the option. For Option No. 2, you would need to contact the national D.A.R.E. headquarters to get the necessary information. You would have to obtain the written approval of both the chief of police and the school superintendent. The police would need to give an officer time off in order to undergo eighty hours of D.A.R.E. training. The schools would have to agree to allot time and space for D.A.R.E. presentations. While the students' D.A.R.E. instruction kits are free the first year, there is a charge for subsequent years. That ongoing cost would have to be covered.

We've seen that most goals can be reached in a variety of ways. Some are obviously more effective than others, but all might work at some time or other. You need to consider each possible path.

Think of your goal as a big bull's-eye target which you must hit dead-center. You have many options to do so. You could choose as Option No. 1 to shoot a rifle at the target. Option No. 2 would see you running to it and throwing a dart at close range. You could, I suppose, have Option No. 3, to bomb it with a water cannon. But you have chosen Option No. 4, to practice archery.

You have lots of arrows (resources) in your quiver. Each arrow has a specific weight, shape, length, and trajectory. You have to select the right arrow to reach the target. Some of the arrows in your quiver will be totally useless for this particular problem, although they might be ideal in another circumstance. You'll want to put them aside for some other use.

Some of the remaining arrows will be too heavy; some will not shoot straight; some will fall short of the target no matter how much tension you put on the bow. Those arrows you'll want to throw far away so no one will be tempted to pick them up and try them out.

Choosing the right arrow is one activity you will need to undertake to hit the bull's-eye.

You also have to choose the right bow—one that will enable you to hit the bull's-eye with the least effort on your part. If the goal is close and large, we might make do with a homemade bow fashioned from an ash tree branch and some kitchen string. But if the target is far away, tiny, and covered with a tough hide, we might want to get a heavy-duty crossbow from the nearest sporting goods store.

So you have your resources (your arrows and your bow) and your target (your goal). You have chosen an option (archery) that would accomplish your goal. Choosing the right bow and the best arrow are activities that got you where you wanted to go—to hit the target. Choosing the right bow and the right arrow are not the goal, they are the means to the goal.

The same is true in implementing your program. *The activity is not the target. The activity is not the resource.* The _activity_ makes best use of the _resources_ to reach the _goal_.

Or think of this process as a pyramid. The base, the wide part of the pyramid, is the full array of the resources you could call upon. The apex, the top point of the pyramid, is the goal. You have several options you could undertake to get to the top. You could just build a scaffold. Or you could cut steps in the stones. Or build an exterior stairway winding around the pyramid to the top. Or you could build a catapult.

For each of these options you would need a specific, and different, set of resources and activities. If you build a stairway, you would need someone to calculate its length and angle, you would need a stone mason to design steps, and you would have to find heavy-duty equipment capable of carving out the stone. If you chose the option to build scaffolding, you would need a partner to plan it and resources such as the lumber or steel to build it.

Some resources you might have could appear to be more decorative (a staircase made of wrought-iron rather than unfinished 2' x 4' lumber) but vital nevertheless. Others may turn out to be quite useless—but useless only in this particular context.

So as you approach your decision, ask yourself these simple questions: What different options would get us to our goal? Which ones of the many viable options make the most sense?

See if you can jot down three options that would work for you to reach your goal. If you can come up with only a couple, OK, but try for three. If you find you have four or more options, see if you can combine two or more, or recognize that one of them is simply not realistic, or whatever. Three options are what you can most easily work with here.

Turn to Exercise 4-2. Remembering your goal, write down three optional ways you might achieve that goal. For each one, summarize briefly why you (or your group) can do this, and what partners and resources you might need.

Options

Write your goal again here.

_____

_____

_____

_____

Now list the three ways (options) you are considering for meeting your goal, and below each one, list three activities that you would need to undertake to fulfill the option.

Option No. 1 _____

    1a _____

        _____

        _____

    1b _____

        _____

        _____

    1c _____

        _____

        _____

Option No. 2 _____

   2a _____

        _____

        _____

   2b _____

        _____

        _____

   2c _____

        _____

        _____

Option No. 3 _____

   3a _____

        _____

        _____

   3b _____

        _____

        _____

   3c _____

        _____

Now look at the options you wrote above. Go to Exercise 4-3. For one of the options, choose one of the three major activities that would be required. Then try to think of the sub-activities that would be required. Don't get too detailed here—just sketch in broad strokes the principal things that you, or someone, would have to undertake. We're not talking about resources here, remember, we're talking about activities.

Depending on your option, certain steps or activities might be mandated. Those required by law should be quite easy to list. Those that are required by custom, or political reality, or religious precepts might be more difficult to document, but relatively straightforward. These are critical activities that you must note. For example:

If you are starting a new non-profit, you will have to incorporate. You will have to find at least three people to serve on your Board of Directors. You will have to file the necessary state and IRS documents.

If you are renovating a dingy senior center, you will have to make provision for handicapped access.

If you are working with teens, you'll need (or want) to have all adults undergo sexual-harassment prevention training.

If any of your activities (or sub-activities) is mandated by law, put a star next to it.

Next to each sub-activity, now note which partner would be responsible. Stating explicitly who would undertake each activity sets up joint accountability. At some point you'll need to rely on others to complete their work. If I am in charge of activity B, which cannot start until activity A is complete, I need to know precisely with whom I need to collaborate. If together we need to accomplish task C, we both need to be clear about our roles. So defining exactly each partner's assignment will smooth the program's operations.

Activities and Resources

Write your goal again here.

_____

_____

_____

_____

_____

Now list one of the options you are considering for meeting your goal.

_____

_____

List one of the activities that you would need to undertake to fulfill

the option. _____

_____

Now list three sub-activities that would be part of the overall activity above.

a _____

_____

_____

b _____

_____

_____

c   _____

_____

_____

[When you finish this part, go back to the text; you'll come here again in a moment to do some more work.]

Now what resources do you need to complete your project? List as many as seem reasonable at this point.

_____

_____

_____

_____

_____

_____

_____

_____

_____

_____

_____

Following this exercise, do a bit of thinking. Consider if you would be the right person or group to carry out each one of these options. Once you have identified the required steps for a particular choice, you might realize that you are not competent to carry it out. Of you suddenly find that the option is just too complicated or too expensive for the amount of resources you have available. Or that a particular option is going to take too much time. If so, drop it from your list of possibilities. Or you might keep that option if you could expand the number of potential partners in order to bring into the mix some other resources you had not thought of originally.

Now we get into resources. What do you need to get the job done? And whom do you need? Do you need counselors, or donations, or folks handy with a hammer and saw? Do you need teachers or writers? Do you need equipment or supplies? Or contacts in high places? What are the essential ingredients—the arrows—that you need to hit your bull's-eye?

Go back to your list of resources. Pull out those that would be most valuable for each of the sub-activities you've listed. And jot them down in Exercise 4-3.

Now go back and do the same exercise (activity, sub-activities, resources) for each of the other options you are considering. At this point you do not need to list every activity that you might undertake to reach each option. Some activities might be non-essential, but nice to do anyhow. You might not need to paint a cheerful mural in the entry hall of that senior center, but you might want to do so, especially if one of your resources is an artist willing to volunteer.

Sometimes two activities would produce the same result, but at different cost. You will have to decide between them. You could hire carpenters or rely on volunteer labor. Carpenters are more expensive but probably quicker and more professional. Volunteers are free but require more oversight and more training. You choose.

So many decisions—can't we just pick one and get on with it? Not so fast, there.

Think about it. If you were going to buy a new sofa, you'd shop around, wouldn't you? You'd compare prices and quality and even delivery times?

You may love that sofa in the specialty shop, but the delivery time is twelve weeks, and you want the sofa in time for your mother-in-law's visit next week. Or you may think the price of that sofa in the big-box store is right-on, but you worry about how well the sofa will last when your three little boys romp on it.

So you investigate, weigh the various options, check out prices and time delays, and finally choose the best sofa for your particular circumstances.

So it is with outreach programs. You need to "shop around." You need to look at your various options and choose the one that fits your need and your purse.

Don't be discouraged right now that this seems too onerous a procedure. Don't worry that this is slowing you down from getting on with the program. This may seem a bit tedious right now, if one of your options is quite obviously the right one. But do it anyway. Trust me here. What we want to find are those activities that will get us to our goal in the most efficient and effective way, at the least cost in the shortest time. Hidden in this analysis may be something that you hadn't considered. You may turn up an even better way of doing good!

Finally, in Exercise 4-4, tell why you should be the leading partner in this program, and then list all the other partners who should be involved in this program. Starting with the beneficiary partner, you need to catalogue every partner you can think of who might participate, and jot down what they might contribute. Which partner or partners would bring essential expertise or resources to each option? You may discover that one of your partners can contribute far more than you initially thought.

Partners

In the space below, describe why you are the right partner (person or group) to *lead* this program.

_____

_____

_____

_____

_____

_____

Now list all the partners you think you *might* need to carry out this program—both those who must be involved, and those who may be useful or want to be involved.

_____

_____

_____

_____

_____

_____

Circle the names of those partners who must be on board if you are to successfully complete this program.

It's important that you don't skip any of these exercises. You may be fairly certain that you know exactly what option is best, with what set of activities and sub-activities, and with which partners using which resources. Go through the exercises anyhow. If it later turns out that you were right all along, won't you feel better knowing that you were proved right? If that happens, you have my permission to tell me: "I told you so!"

Remember, we're learning a new way to approach outreach. We are trying to get away from the idea of throwing money at a problem, willy-nilly, and hoping that some of it sticks enough to make a difference. We're learning the best-practices of the most successful outreach organizations. We're breaking old habits (we all know how hard that can be) in order to learn a better way. In order to do that, we need to break down the decision process into its component parts.

Later on, you'll find that you automatically process these steps whenever you encounter a problem to be solved. The brightest and best outreach planners run through these steps every time they need to choose a new intervention. The process becomes second nature to them. For simple projects, they might do the exercise without even consciously thinking about it. But for more complex problems, you can be assured that they follow extremely rigorous procedures. They want to be as certain as they can be that whatever option they choose will do the job.

Think of commercial airline pilots. Before each and every flight they follow a written, detailed preflight checklist to be certain that no critical steps are inadvertently missed. The pilot may have done this safeguard review hundreds, or thousands, of times. No matter. The pilot still consciously checks off each item on the checklist. Forgetting even one small detail could spell disaster.

You will want to be sure, too, that you do not overlook even one small aspect of your plan. While you might not "crash" if you miss one, you can increase your chances of success if you walk through the steps. So hang in there. Walk with me. You'll discover an easy and sensible way to make your outreach decision.

    ∞ *An international development organization wanted to rebuild the economy in war-torn Kosovo. Among the alternatives they considered were rebuilding shops in the commercial center of a small town, setting up a trade school to train teenagers to service computers, and rebuilding and upgrading the quality of the beef cattle (the primary economic activity in the rural areas).*

They chose the latter option even though they knew they had neither the expertise nor the skills to implement it. The resource they had in abundance, however, were donations earmarked for "development programs in Kosovo."

The agency put out an RFP (Request For Proposal) to other nonprofit agencies, which responded with their plans to meet the goal. Several different activities were proposed: importing bulls and heifers of better breeding stock, training the farmers in better management skills, establishing new breeds that might be better suited to the terrain and the available feedstock.

The final decision, however, was a program of artificial insemination to upgrade the quality of the cattle. Among the steps that had to be accomplished were training for the local veterinarians, supplying gas-powered refrigerators for the semen, providing the equipment necessary for the impregnation, and granting subsidies to the veterinarians for their travel.

Among the partners that the organization included was of course, the implementing partner, but also the Kosovo veterinary organization, the local agricultural experts, and a sample group of the Kosovo farmers. ⌀

The organization saw a need, explored options, catalogued its resources, examined potential partners, and chose the activity that would best meet the goal.

But more than likely, you'll come up with two or three alternatives that seem to make sense. You'll recognize that you have a couple (or maybe even more) of roads to your destination. Automobile GPSs are programmed to allow you to choose between the shortest route to your destination, or the fastest. (I hope that someday they add a third option: the most scenic—wouldn't that be nice?) Some GPSs allow you an additional option—up-to-the-minute information on traffic congestion to allow you to choose an alternate route.

In the case of outreach options, we might have the lowest-cost but longest-timeline version, the higher-cost but quickly done version, and something in between. Or we might have the all-volunteer version versus the all-hired-help version. Or we might have the version that has the fewest components in order to simplify our program and avoid that "congestion."

In a moment we are going to look at a grid that provides another way to view your various options and come to a clear decision. Making such a grid is particularly useful if you are part of a group trying to come to a decision. In most cases, individuals have an easier time selecting from among the various options on the table than a group does. Once you start bringing several people to the table of options, of course, you start bringing other opinions. Once you start operating as a committee, the dynamics and the processes change.

Committees are great—they bring together various experiences, viewpoints, and skills. The old saying "Two heads are better than one" expands exponentially—three are nine times better, six are . . . well, you get the point. But you need a way to harness all that talent. And we need to recognize that too many participants may make a many-headed Hydra. Include all those you need for your committee decision-making process, for sure, but limit participation to those who truly have something to offer.

Another saying can also be true: "A camel is a horse designed by a committee." We don't want a plodding, ill-shaped camel as our program; we want a sleek, swift horse. Putting ourselves through a formal exercise keeps us on the racetrack instead of in the desert caravan.

I RESENT THAT REMARK!

Now let's turn to that grid. If you are undertaking this project yourself, you will be able to make your own grid in only a few minutes. If you are a member of a committee, we suggest that each person complete the grid alone, and then ask the entire committee to take a few minutes to compare answers and develop a consolidated grid. You'll be amazed at how closely each person's grid matches that of the others.

As you look at our sample grid, you will see across the bottom from left to right an axis labeled "mandated vs. nice to do." The vertical axis is the cost, with least cost on the bottom, and greatest cost at the top. Take a moment to review this grid now. Then move on to Exercise 4-5 to develop a sample based on your responses in Exercises 4-2 and 4-3.

Cost Analysis of Essential vs. Nice-to-Do Activities

Look carefully at the dispersion of the activities of each of the options numbers 1, 2, and 3. The vertical axis shows the relative "cost" of the activity (either in dollars or in volunteer commitment—however you choose to denominate it). Here we are considering monetary cost. The horizontal axis shows how essential each activity is to the completion of the project. Note that the letters following the option number indicate the "essential-ness" of each of the activities: "a" indicating the most essential; "g" indicating the least.

High Cost	1a							2e	2f
			1d						3b
		1b						3c	
			2d						
	3a							3d	
			2b	3f		2g			
	1c				1g				
Low Cost	2a		2c	3e		3g			

Essential   **Nice-to-Do**

You can see that Option 1 has three relatively essential activities, one of them at very high cost, the other two at somewhat lower cost. It also has a fourth nearly essential element at a very high cost. It has only one nice-to-do item.

Option 2 has only one essential activity, and at a very low cost. However, Option 2 has three less essential but important elements, one of which is moderately expensive, and two nice-to-do items at high cost.

Option 3 has one essential activity, at a moderate cost. It then has two more elements at the mid-point on the essentialness axis; it and all but one of the remaining activities cluster in the low-cost, nice-to-do area.

If money is no object, any of these options would suffice. But if the budget is tight, you would probably want to settle on Option 3, which has the fewest high-cost essential elements. As money became available, the remaining nice-to-do activities could be undertaken. You could choose to do only one high-cost activity, perhaps 3b, or, for the same amount of money, undertake both activities 3d and 3g.

Now, let's try making your own chart. In Exercise 4-5, you will enter the activities and sub-activities you worked up in Exercises 4-2 and 4-3. Number them so that: Option No. 1, Activity "a" would be 1a on the chart; Option No. 3, Activity "c" would be 3c, and so forth. You may even want to color code them: Green for Option No. 1 activities, red for Option No. 2, and so forth.

Estimate how vital the activity is to the completion of the project (across the bottom axis) and then estimate its cost on the vertical axis (don't worry about precise numbers—what we are looking for here are relative costs). When you finish, you should have a graphic illustration that shows you the distribution of mandated, essential, and "nice-to-do" activities for each option, compared to each other option. Remember that mandated activities generally (though not always) are more expensive and time-consuming than the essential or even the "nice" activities. If you have limited time and money, you might want to take that reality into account.

You will be able to see, from the clustering of activities, which options require the most essential activities. At the same time, you can see which of these activities are the most costly. If Option No. 2's essential activities cluster in the high-cost section of the graph, you might want to choose that one if you had more money than time or expertise. The low-cost activities will likely be those where most of the work is done by volunteers, although not always. Be sure that you have access to enough volunteer labor and talent to keep the option on the table. If not, discard it now as impractical.

Finally, you can clearly see what activities are "nice to do"—but not essential to the goal—whether they be high- or low-cost, and remove them from your consideration. For now, we must focus only on what we have to do to get the project done, not what we would like to do to make it more interesting, more beautiful, or whatever. That can come later.

Creating Your Own Cost-Analysis

Enter the activities and sub-activities you worked up in Exercises 4-2 and 4-3. Number them so that Option No. 1, Activity "a" would be 1a on the chart; Option No. 3, Activity "c" would be 3c, etc. Estimate how vital the activity is, ranging from required/essential to "nice-to-do."

High Cost

Low Cost

Essential   **Nice-to-Do**

Now that you've completed Exercise 4-5, we've reached an appropriate place for a reality check. Keep in mind that old bugaboo, the danger of unintended consequences. What are undoubtedly good works may exacerbate other problems. Solving one problem may simply create another, and perhaps more serious, problem. Every solution has the potential to raise new problems. For example, building new houses for those whose homes were destroyed in an earthquake may raise issues of jealously among those who are stuck with their still-standing but old houses. Providing higher-education scholarships for orphaned children of parents who died of AIDS may ignore some equally worthy students just because their parents were not so afflicted. Unintended consequences can create new, unanticipated problems.

Take a few minutes and pull out that old brainstorming routine. Try to imagine what unintended consequences your options might generate. Who might be hurt? What new problem might be created? How might this option affect your ability to undertake new programs? Will it use up all the talent and goodwill you can muster? Whose toes might you step on, and would it be worth it? Remember the brainstorming rule: We want to get every idea on the table, whether or not it has any obvious merit at this point.

Then sort through the results of your brainstorming. Find all unintended consequences that truly matter. And deal with them. Find ways to meet them, get around them, or, as a final result, if they are too overwhelming, pick another option.

Remember old Murphy's Law? What can go wrong will go wrong? I love some of the corollaries to Murphy's Law:

> *What can go wrong will go wrong . . .*
> *. . . at the most inopportune time.*
> *. . . and it will be all your fault, and everyone will know it.*
> *And if anything simply cannot go wrong, it will anyway.*

But back to business. Don't be discouraged or throw up your hands. This process shouldn't be depressing. Think of it as a game. Just take time to guess what might go wrong. Once you've done that, you can build preventive steps into your plans.

Now is the proper time to bring your partners formally into the project. You have been consulting them all along, haven't you? I do hope that you have included them in your investigations and your brainstorming. If you plan to involve other organizations, they need to be part of your formal planning from here on out. You may be counting on them for resources—be sure they know that. You might be planning to tap their volunteer pool—be sure they agree. Talk with them. Review the exercises you have completed. Undoubtedly they will be able to offer some additional information and some good advice. Keep them in the loop. Keep them informed. Make a special effort to include them, and you'll reap big rewards.

DOCUMENT NO.4
The Timeline

We have only one more element to take into our decision process. That component is Time. We need to know when to start the program and how long it is going to take. We talked about this at length in Chapter 3, under the Journalistic Approach.

For each option you are still considering, you need to know when you would begin the project and have some idea of how long it might take. (Here's the point that the *When?* begins to play its role.)

Some projects are extremely simple, with an obvious solution. Most of those can be accomplished quite quickly. For those, you can probably estimate quite accurately how long the project would take. Other, more complex, programs are longer-term and more prone to delay. See if you can ball-park in your mind the time requirement of each option: a few days, a week, a month, several years?

A timeline document will show the key points along the way to your goal. Here's a sample to get you started. It shows a timeline for building a playground. After you've reviewed it, go to Exercise 4-6 to learn how to construct your own.

Playground Timeline
(Sample of a Simple Schedule)

Define problem and solution in writing		Write "case" statement		Prepare skills needed budget				
	Investigate possible playground sites		Prepare draft budget		Refine budget			
		Obtain pre-approval from nursing home			Sign MOU with nursing home			
	Check liability issues: Construction period and on-going				Go/no go decision point	Set installation date		
			Begin fundraising					
				Recruit volunteers			Schedule workers	
		Locate playground designer and set fee		Obtain material donations				
			Investigate type and cost of playground equipment		Order equipment			
						Plan installation publicity		Write program-end evaluation and final report
Month 1	Month 2	Month 3	Month 4	Month 5	Month 6	Month 7	Month 8	Month 9

Now here's how to construct your own timeline, for each of your options. Using the blank form given in Exercise 4-6, mark off along the bottom line the time periods that best reflect the possible duration of your project. Some projects can be "Done in a Day," as the Junior League of the City of New York labels its high-intensity short-term community service projects. (Obviously, the planning for the "Done in a Day" project starts weeks before the actual event, so the timeline should reflect the true time period.)

Other programs will require weeks, or months, or even years. Use a scale on the timeline that best suits the probable duration of your program.

Then try, as best you can, to estimate just when each one of your planned activities should start and finish. Some can't start until others are complete. You'll need to note this. Some can be accomplished simultaneously. You'll need to know this as well.

What you are developing is a simplified version of the Critical Path Method of project management (but don't let that serious-sounding phrase throw you off course). Using the information developed in the grid, you can figure out just how long the entire project should take, and the timing of each activity to keep you on schedule. This will also show you which elements have to be completed in a particular order (in other words, they can't be started until a previous element is complete)—called the "critical path"—and which can be started earlier or delayed without affecting other activities.

Adding up the total time of the critical path activities will tell you the overall duration of the program—the shortest time possible to complete the project. Any delay in any of these elements will delay the project completion. A project can have several, parallel, critical paths that link up at some later point.

Sometimes a critical path activity can be speeded up by adding resources, or slowed down by shifting resources to another part of the program.

Pay particular attention to mandated activities. Some of these will dictate the pace of the project. You couldn't start construction on a new senior center until you got zoning clearance, for example. Other mandated activities (planning for handicapped access in the senior center) can be incorporated right into the design and shouldn't slow up the timeline.

The required time for decisions made by persons not directly involved in your project can be the most difficult to estimate. Your best defense is to test the waters before proceeding. Get informal buy-in from those on the decision-making body before you undertake the program and rely on their estimate of the time frame. That usually works, but not always. Be prepared, always, for surprises. No matter how much homework you've done, no matter how many folks you've brought into the project and consulted with, no matter what issues you think you've identified and dealt with, unexpected stumbling blocks can always crop up.

> ∞ *A church in a suburban town near New York City was well known for its community-service programs. It hosted several AA meetings a week. The Boy Scouts met there. It opened its doors for First Night programs. It hosted classical music concerts. It ran an exemplary pre-school utilized by parents from across the religious spectrum.*
>
> *The church developed plans to build a new education wing on property that it owned. The new wing would obviously serve the needs of the congregation, but also would expand the church's ability to host community programs and events. It would enable the church to undertake more outreach programs. Its design would enhance the attractiveness of the downtown area.*
>
> *Sounds like a no-brainer, right?*
>
> *Wrong. Turns out, the property on which the wing would be constructed had, at some time in the past, been zoned "residential," even though it was, and had always been, a church parking lot. No one knew this until the church applied for zoning permission to put a building on that site.*
>
> *Months and months of negotiation ensued. In anticipation of a favorable ruling, eventually, the church continued to raise money for the new building. Pledges rolled in. The capital fund-drive was almost complete.*
>
> *Then the great stock-market crash of 2008 happened. Fundraising screeched to a halt. Legitimate concerns were raised about the number of persons who might not be able to fulfill their campaign pledges. The zoning application still had not been approved, though no one seemed to be opposed to the project. The bureaucracy just moved at molasses speed. The church quietly scaled back its plans to go ahead with some of the smaller parts of the plan that could be built on the actual church site (not part of the zoning dilemma). ∞*

So some mandated activities or unexpected situations can throw sand in the best-oiled program. Beware, and be ready for those surprises. Most are not nearly so devastating as the perfect storm of surprises (zoning, stock market crash) that the church had to weather. But surprises do happen, and we can better meet them if we know to watch for them.

You've heard: Forewarned is forearmed? That is as true in project management as in any other situation.

As I am writing this, my town is under a tornado watch. Thank goodness for technological advances and better understanding of weather—now we know when possible tornado weather is approaching, and can prepare to take shelter. When I was a child growing up on a farm on the prairie in Nebraska, all we could do was scan the clouds for ugly looking funnels. Because we had no tornado-warning devices, we had to be constantly on the alert during tornado season. Now I can relax unless the alarm sounds or The Weather Channel tells me to watch out. Forewarned is forearmed, we're told. That's true in weather-watches; it is also true in outreach programming.

So be on the alert for those surprises, but be forearmed by anticipating as many of them as you can.

If you are still deliberating between two or more options, you'll want to prepare a critical path chart for each. These charts should give you a much clearer picture of the time required to finish the project, the possible points where you might get hung-up waiting for other decisions or activities, and places where you can, maybe by using additional resources, undertake several activities at the same time.

You may find that one option simply takes more time and sustained interest than you think your group can maintain. One option may take too long given the urgency of the problem. A different option might just be too weighted down with mandated activities.

Conversely, another option may allow for a quick start with few or no decisions outside your control. You may be able to undertake several activities simultaneously. You may zip across your timeline in record time.

Making Your Timeline— Completing a Critical Path Grid

Select the appropriate time period, such as week, month, quarter, and list them across the bottom of this chart. Then list activities than can or must be accomplished during each time period.

Period 1	Period 2	Period 3	Period 4	Period 5	Period 6

Once you have listed the options, then the activities that would support each option, the possible partners and the resources that would be required, and the time frame to complete it, some options will clearly drop out. Some are just not possible. Some will be downright laughable (at least we hope so, if you have done your brainstorming).

Hurrah! We're almost there.

DOCUMENT NO. 5
The Budget

All programs cost something. Most cost money. Most cost time, often volunteer but more frequently these days, paid staff or workers. Most cost other resources.

To be sure that all parties understand what resources are needed to make the project successful, you should develop a written budget. You don't need an accountant or a CPA to do this—you know how. This is not a document that will be audited by the IRS. This is a working document to guide you, to help in future decision making. A good budget should help you maximize resources. It should help you stay on track. It should also help you evaluate the benefits of your program later on.

By now you have probably narrowed down your decision to two or three viable options. The last step in deciding is to calculate what each of the requisite activities in each option would cost. (Right now we're using cost to mean hard cold cash. But you know by now that you can often substitute talent and volunteer time for dollars.)

In order to manage your project carefully, you'll need to prepare a cash budget—in writing. You should try to anticipate every possible expenditure. Look at each activity in your plan; try to think of all conceivable costs to achieve it. Don't forget supplies, or postage, or the cost of tools. Don't rely on vague promises of donated materials—be grateful if you get them, but don't count on them. (One major exception to that last rule: If your project is more than fifty percent dependent upon donated materials, then you have to rely on the promise that those donations will come through. Otherwise, you really don't have a viable project.)

Brainstorming can come in handy here too. Or find people who are knowledgeable about your particular kind of project. They need not be participants in the project. In fact, these resource people are often more valuable if they are not going to be part of the project. They can be more objective. They will not bring with them any biases. They will want you to succeed, but they will surely want to give you advice that will prevent your stumbling unaware into unseen expenses.

These "experts" would probably be delighted to meet with you on a one-shot basis to help you ferret out every possible cost. For example, if you are planning to renovate a run-down storage shed for your church's food-bank supplies, ask a local housing developer, or owner of a lumber yard, or an architect who can identify costs that you might have overlooked. If you are starting a new program at the senior center, you might gather a group that includes a social worker and a physician specializing in geriatric health. They work with this population all the time and can recognize where you may have under- or over-estimated some of your costs.

As you forecast the costs of your program, remember the old saying that things always cost more than we think (as well as taking longer than we expect). So, in general, gently err on the side of overestimating. You'll get applause if you bring in the project under-budget. On the other hand, no one is going to sing your praises if you have to go back to the donors for more money. In fact, the tune you hear is likely to be decidedly off-key!

In addition to generous estimates of the cost of each project component, be sure that you build in a healthy contingency fund—for those unexpected and unavoidable expenses that seem always to crop up. Ten to fifteen percent of the itemized budget is usually a good rule of thumb—you can use the lower percentage for simple, short-term, low-cost projects, and the higher one for longer, more complicated projects. The more parts to the project, the greater chance you'll have to deal with overruns in both cost and time. Remember that time overruns generally simply mean the project will be completed later, but cost overruns generally increase exponentially. A small cost overrun early in the project is likely to build to a large cost overrun at the end of the project. So be exceptionally wary of cost issues in the early stages of the program.

You should also prepare a "budget" that includes as "income" all anticipated donated resources: volunteer time, donated goods, physical space. It should then apportion those assets among the various activities you plan. You may find that you are very well off indeed, with plenty of assets from which to choose. More often, unfortunately, you will find that you are short in some area. The "donations" budget process will help you match your needs with your resources.

This budget process will enable you to be sure—before you start—that you know where all your resources are going to come from, or how or where you are going to get those that you do not yet have. Beware of promises or pledges of support. These have a habit of disappearing when conditions change. (Remember the story of the church expansion project that faltered in the wake of the economic downturn of 2008?)

So if you are going to rely on pledges or promises or fundraising campaigns, be especially conservative in your estimation. We suggest you discount your pledges or proposed fundraising income by fifty percent—if you have one hundred dollars in pledges, we suggest that you include only fifty dollars in your income budget. If you get more than that, great! But if you include all one hundred and some of it falls through, you are in a difficult situation.

You are probably going to have to do some fundraising. If you have done all the exercises in the previous chapters, you are going to be well-positioned for effective fundraising. You've already done all the hard work. The two most important elements of a good fundraising approach are an urgent need and a well-thought-out plan to meet it. With these elements in place, you are prepared to approach individuals, foundations, corporations, or governmental agencies for funding.

Your analysis of your goal has given you the information you need to describe an urgent need. If the problem that you plan to address is not urgent, is not a pressing need, why bother? So look carefully again at that goal setting material and state the need you have uncovered—but state it in such a way that the hearer will understand that this problem needs to be addressed right now!

Next, the plans you have developed; the activities you will undertake, with what resources and partners, at what time and how, will constitute your remedy. In fundraising lingo, this is called your "case" or "case statement."

The case need not be overly detailed. Give the reader just enough information to substantiate that you know what you are going to do and what you are going to achieve—when, and at what cost.

And then ask for the money.

The biggest mistake novice fundraisers make is being afraid to actually ask for the money. So they hedge and fritter and say such namby-pamby things as, "Could you help us?" or "Read this and call me if you have any questions."

Instead, the only way to get what you want is to ask for it. Remember your letters to Santa Claus? Remember how you worried over the list of the presents that you wanted? Maybe you did, but I never said, "Santa, I hope you'll bring me something."

In asking for the money, you can say something like, "Could you consider giving this program a donation of $x?" or "Is there some portion of this program that you would like to fund?" Note that you have not directly asked for any particular amount. You have suggested an amount (and don't be afraid of asking for too much—no one has ever been offended when people thought they were more wealthy than they really were). Donors are perfectly capable of giving whatever amount makes sense to them.

> ∞ *The best illustration of this I know actually happened when I was a fundraising staff member at a major hospital. Our research had suggested that a donor who had given about ten thousand dollars each year could probably give a very large, one-time contribution. Over a period of several months, we sent him all kinds of information about the hospital, took him on tours, introduced him to the hospital president, set up a luncheon for him with the Board chairman, and so forth.*
>
> *Finally, it was time for the big ask. We selected the head of one of the hospital departments to ask our prospective donor for enough money (over three hundred thousand dollars) to complete a new laboratory. Needless to say, the department head was extremely nervous. I reassured him before he departed for the meeting, and on a whim,*

suggested he ask the prospective donor also to support the ongoing costs of the lab for twenty years. "How much would that be," the soliciting person asked? "Oh, about a million dollars a year, give or take," I calculated.

Immediately after the department head met with the donor, he called me. He had the donor's personal check for the entire cost of the laboratory in his pocket, and a pledge of one million dollars per year for the next twenty years. ❧

If you don't ask, you don't get. Remember that.

This has been a quick overview of basic fundraising principles. If you want to learn more, there are many good books out there. You might also be able to find a retired professional fundraiser to volunteer to lead you. With all those other organizations out there raising funds, you need to be as competent as you can possibly be. Don't shortchange this step if you need to raise funds for your program.

In order to avoid some unpleasant and unfruitful mistakes, we've included below a few of the fundraising myths that persist out there. Read them, laugh a bit at them, and learn from them.

Myth No. 1:

We'll just ask Joe; he's got lots of money.

We think that Joe is wealthy because he drives an expensive new car, lives in a lovely big home, and belongs to the country club. What we didn't know was that Joe's car is leased, his house is mortgaged, and his country club membership is paid for by his company, which is on the verge of bankruptcy.

Or maybe what we didn't know was that Joe is supporting three members of his extended family, has a large student loan that he is paying off slowly, and has had extremely large dental bills recently.

Or maybe what we didn't know was that Joe has absolutely no interest in supporting our cause—and that he is actually a major contributor to another philanthropic venture.

Myth No. 2:

We'll just ask everyone to give their fair share—we have to raise one thousand dollars; we have a thousand members, so we'll just ask everyone to give one dollar.

In reality, not everyone will or can give. The old fundraising rule used to be that you will get eighty percent of your money from twenty percent of your donors. Lately, organizations have been reporting their experience is closer to getting ninety percent of their money from ten percent of their donors. Using a per-donor calculation will get you into trouble every time.

Myth No. 3:

Organization X in our town reported that they raised one hundred thousand dollars at their fundraising dinner dance, so let's do the same thing, and we'll raise a similar amount.

Maybe you will, but did you ask how much Organization X spent on that dinner dance? In other words, maybe they had income in that amount, but how much did they clear after they paid all expenses? Most fundraising events of that nature are lucky if they clear twenty percent after expenses. And they are generally a lot of work—a big investment of volunteer resources.

Secondly, is your constituency the same as the other organization? If your constituency is the beer and pretzels type, and the other organization is the champagne and caviar type, you're going to have very different results with the same program.

Fundraising events can be successful in raising dollars, but they are more often used as "friend-raisers" and to identify people who could later become major donors to your program.

(By the way, don't make a common mistake. Federal law requires that you notify donors how much of the ticket price is a charitable donation. The charitable donation portion of the event price is calculated as that amount over the amount of "value received" by the purchaser. If the event price is one hundred dollars and the purchaser receives a dinner worth fifty dollars, the charitable donation is fifty dollars. This is true even if the cost of the event was underwritten by another donor.)

Myth No. 4:

We sent our donors a form-letter thank you. That's enough.

It is, if you don't care if they ever contribute again. Good donor relations suggest that you find seven—yes, seven—ways to thank a donor. Perhaps you won't want to go to this extreme effort for a donor who sends in a smaller check (although doing so would be a good thing if you suspect that person has the capability to make a really large donation), but if you want to increase your "donor retention" you certainly should do so for major donors.

You can easily think of seven ways to thank someone: the formal acknowledgement, a handwritten note from the chairman, a phone call from the president or a board member, a short program update from the person implementing the program, and so on. Not all thank-yous have to be sent in the first few weeks.

Remember, the rule of thumb is that of those who give to you once, only fifty percent will give to you again unless you make some additional effort. You want to up that percentage in any way you can. Thanking people is a superb start.

We're sure you can probably add some other myths to this list—they abound out there. If you are new to fundraising, beware. But don't let the possibility of making a mistake stop you. No mistake is fatal. And if you don't try, you won't succeed.

Because you will expect donations to arrive during various times in your project, you should also prepare a brief cash-flow statement. Even if you have all the cash you need in hand at the beginning, a cash-flow statement will be an important project management tool. It will tell you if you are spending the amounts you expected to, and when you expected to. It will enable you to adjust programs should some element cost more (or possibly less) than projected.

Cash-flow analyses differ from budgets. Budgets tell you how much money you expect from each source (your income) and how much money you'll need (your expenditures). Ideally, your income and your expenditures will balance. (If not, you need to adjust somewhere.)

Cash-flow charts, on the other hand, tell you *when* you expect additional income, and *when* each major expenditure will occur. On the income side, you should count up what funds you have in hand, and guesstimate when additional funds will be forthcoming. You probably won't have all your money right at the beginning (although that is a wonderful way to be able to begin a project). At the same time, you probably won't need all your money at the beginning, so you must plan when you will need more cash. Whether you have funds now in hand, or plan to acquire more during the life of the program, you should try to estimate your income cash-flow. Be conservative. Money frequently doesn't arrive when expected or promised. Build in some leeway.

On the expense side, you should calculate how much you will need to start, when you will need more money, and how much. You will need to know how much money you need at each stage of the program, and for which activity. Some cash you will need in order to get started. Other money you won't need for a long time. So you need to know at which step, at which time, you will need to spend more money.

The cash-flow chart will show you clearly whether your income and expenditures match up or not throughout the project. You will need to know which and how many resources you need at each stage of the program, and for which activity. Here, too, be conservative! Overestimate your expenditures and underestimate your income. That's the safe way— the better way. Beware of those saying, "We hope to get . . . ." All too often, they don't.

For projects involving volunteers, you'll also want to prepare a volunteer "budget" and a work-flow chart. How many volunteers will you need (with what talents) and when? Do you have enough volunteers at the right time? How will they be managed and deployed? And how will they be "paid?" Be sure to plan for lots of ways to say thanks, to salute their contributions. We're pretty good about formally thanking people for their monetary donations (and under IRS rules, non-profits are required to send a formal acknowledgement for every contribution over two hundred fifty dollars). But we often get too busy to say thank you to those who contribute their time and their talent. So build those recognition moments right into your work-flow chart.

Let's look at how one organization looked at its cash-flow needs.

    ∽ *The organization's goal was to improve the nutrition of rural people in remote mountainous regions of El Salvador. First, they had to discover what was missing in the people's diet—turned out it was protein. But what kind of protein would be most suitable? They had to first determine what kinds of protein-producing activities they might undertake.*

So a Spanish-speaking staff member flew (airfare cost, right?) to El Salvador to talk with the local people (the beneficiary partners). Based on that discussion, the two partners decided to undertake a poultry project, as chickens are useful for both eggs and, ultimately, the stew pot.

The organization hired (salary cost) a local, Spanish-speaking poultry expert to train the beneficiaries in managing and caring for their flocks. Other partners—agricultural ministers and local political leaders—needed to be brought into the discussion (primarily out-of-pocket expense for travel and entertainment). The local partners filed the necessary papers and obtained the concurrence of the local authorities. During this time the staff made several trips back and forth to El Salvador to iron out details of the program (more airfares and hotel costs).

The organization paid for the local poultry expert to attend some refresher classes. They paid him for his time spent in preparing the training course and doing the actual training. They also paid for supplies: workbooks, veterinary supplies, and the like.

They paid the students a small stipend for their time spent attending classes. Only after all this activity did the students actually need to buy chickens. To get fuzzy baby chicks at the beginning of the project would be starting at the wrong end, wouldn't it? ∽

Such poultry projects can have magnificent results. Here's a real-life example:

> ❧ After the civil war in El Salvador, many of the ex-combatants had a difficult time reintegrating into their communities. One of these men was extremely depressed—sullen and uncooperative—ignoring the needs of his family, which was sinking into poverty.
>
> A U.S.-based international development organization and its local partners were sponsoring a poultry project nearby. Now, raising chickens in El Salvador is difficult—they have to be penned to protect them from predators, vaccinated twice a year to prevent avian cholera, and fed a special diet. But poultry are also excellent and inexpensive sources of protein, generally lacking in the typical Salvadoran diet.
>
> The partners convinced him that this program would work for him. After training in their care and feeding, he received ten hens and two roosters.
>
> Only a couple of years later, his ten hens and two roosters had multiplied like the loaves and fishes. He had built a three-story chicken-house condominium out of bamboo and chicken wire for his fifty or sixty laying hens. Behind the condo, a penned area held what must have been another fifty or sixty small chickens, on their way to occupying either the laying condo or the cooking pot!
>
> But then he recognized the potential from all that poultry manure. So he cleared an area of about an acre behind his house. He tilled the soil, worked the fertilizer into it, and installed a drip irrigation system fed by a hand-cranked wheel attached to his open well.
>
> On that acre, he was growing the most beautiful tomatoes and peppers. He sold them, and the surplus eggs and chickens, in the local markets. The entire local community benefitted from his effort.
>
> When representatives of the development organization visited his successful chicken ranch, he shook their hands and declared that this was the first time he has ever had hope for his family. He and his family had recovered their dignity and their future. They now had new lives, free of poverty and famine. ❧

The budget prepared by this implementing organization was comprehensive, covering all possible costs for the program. The cash-flow analysis provided information as to when money would be needed. The program was brought in on-time, on-budget. The beneficiary partners had plenty of protein in their diets from then on, improving their general health. Therefore the program was a success from everyone's point of view.

Now you have your budget (or budgets if you are still wavering between two or more options) and your cash-flow analyses. You know, as best you can right now, just what this project is going to cost you, in hard cold cash. You know when you are going to need to spend money. You know when you are going to get more money, and from whom.

Do you have enough information? If so, fantastic. Get on with it! Make your decision and get ready to start.

If so, you can skip the next paragraph.

If, however, your cash-flow analysis shows significant shortfalls, where are you going to get the rest of the necessary funds? And when? Don't be a whimsical dreamer here. Face reality. Fundraising events often fall short of their goals, and they, too, are subject to unanticipated costs. Pledges of funds can be withdrawn, or simply not honored. Those "sure-thing" grants turn out to be not so sure after all. Government funds suddenly get cut by a new administration (local, state, or federal). The 2008 economic implosion had significant adverse effects on many, many programs across the country, not just the church-building project described above.

If you are not fully confident of your funding, you may have to alter your plans. You can either scale back your program to a manageable size, pick your second-place option, or you can undertake the program in steps, as funds become available.

> ∽ When The Church of St. Luke in the Fields, the third oldest
> Episcopal Church in New York City, burned down in 1981, the rector
> and the vestry vowed to rebuild, starting as soon as the charred
> debris was cleared. However, they also stipulated that they would
> continue rebuilding only so long as they had in hand the cash to
> cover the costs.
>
> Contributions came pouring in at first, and slowly the new church
> began rising from the ashes. Then, one Sunday, after church services
> in the gym of the adjacent parochial school, the parishioners asked

the rector why no work had been done on the building during the previous week. "No money, no work," sighed the rector.

Not surprisingly, new contributions arrived at the church office early the next week. And so it went, start and stop, build and wait, depending upon the flow of funds. Desire to get the church building completed led to some extremely creative fundraising efforts. One of the most memorable was an eleven-year-old student at the church's school who played her violin on the street corner to raise money for the building fund. With energy and enthusiasm like this, the church rededicated the finished building in record time—without borrowing a dime. ❧

Obviously, this method isn't always possible. Had the burned building been a hospital, for example, rebuilding would have had to begin immediately. But St. Luke's experience shows us one way to meet the challenge of a project that we know will be more expensive than our current funds can support. Having tangible proof of the use of their donations, right in front of their eyes, kept the congregation focused on the need for additional funds.

Stop for just a minute. You've created quite a series of documents, haven't you? You've done good work. You know what you are trying to accomplish, where, when, and with whom. You know what your costs are going to be, in money and in donated services and supplies. You know how long your project is going to take, and the sequence of activities that will be required. You know when major expenditures will occur and that you should be able to fund them at that time.

At this point, you need to boil all this down into one one-page document. We could call it a "contract," but that would be a little too formal and legalistic for our purposes. We prefer to call it a "mutual commitment" or more often, a "memorandum of understanding," an MOU.

DOCUMENT NO. 6
The MOU—The Memorandum of Understanding

I suppose I could think of a program that required no partners—a go-it-alone, do-it-yourself project. Perhaps your goal was to enhance the attractiveness of your neighborhood. You might decide the most needed activity was maintaining litter-free roadsides in your neighborhood. So once a week you went out and picked up all the debris yourself. You'd certainly make your neighbors happy, and you might increase the potential sale value of yours and nearby homes. That would be a program you could carry out with no partners.

(But why? Why not include your neighbors as partners? They may enjoy being part of a community activity, and you would need them to carry on if, perchance, you broke your leg or were suddenly inundated at work. And if they want to sell their home at a better price, they should invest some time in making the neighborhood attractive.)

But as you get into more complicated programs, your program will undoubtedly require partners. Sometimes the program will require only two partners, you and a beneficiary partner. Usually the program will require that you add other partners: donors of monetary resources, those with special expertise or resources, governmental bodies with control over some portion of the process. Sometimes a program becomes so complex that you need partners to assume total responsibility for one of the required activities, all of which will contribute to the final goal.

But no matter how many partners you have, no matter what the role of each partner, you need a Memorandum of Understanding with each of them. The MOU should state clearly the goal of the program, the activities to be carried out, what each partner will contribute, what is expected of each partner, and when. The MOU should name the person in charge and detail that person's responsibilities and authority.

Although one might think this is just asking for trouble, we recommend that you outline how differences of opinion will be settled. Better to be prepared than have to work through controversy when tempers might be a bit warm and suspicions might be lurking. After all, we are all human, no matter what our good intentions are.

The MOU does not need to be a legal document. It does not need to be off-putting. Drafting an MOU will often raise important questions, and settle future controversies. Making an MOU an integral part of your plan does not imply distrust or doubts about your partners. Properly presented, all parties will agree that having an MOU signed before the project begins is a wise idea.

The MOU will summarize all the salient points of the project. Its purpose is to ensure that all parties to the project have the same understanding. Now is the time to spot any misunderstandings. Now is the time to pinpoint missed expectations. The MOU will define each party's role and responsibility.

Sometimes we are astounded at how many different interpretations surface during the writing of the MOU. "I didn't know I was going to be responsible for that!" "We never agreed to do that!" "Our group can't raise that kind of money."

Better to unravel these discrepancies right now rather than later on, in the middle of the project.

On the next page you'll find a sample MOU for a simple project. A more complex one would differ only in number of details, not format. They would both cover the same ground. Both would enumerate the resources that each party will provide. Both would estimate the time required to complete the project. Both would refer to attached documents providing more planning detail, such as budgets and cash-flow analyses. Both would require all parties to sign.

We have given you a blank form to help you get started writing your own MOU. At this point, with all you have accomplished up to this point, writing the MOU should almost be fun. (I know, some of us have a rather warped sense of humor!) But there it will be, on one sheet of paper, the proof of all your hard work to date.

Once you have the finalized MOU, once each party has signed it, signifying a mutual commitment to the other parties, you have a deal. You have made your decision. You have a program to solve a problem. You're on your way to making a real difference to someone somewhere in the world. Congratulations!

MEMORANDUM OF UNDERSTANDING

July 9, 2009

This memorandum of understanding (MOU) spells out the responsibilities of the following parties to a program to landscape and plant perennial flower gardens along the walkway in front of the Anywhere Public Library.

By August 1, 2009, the Library will provide the area to be planted, which is the three-foot border on either side of the current walkway from the street to the front steps of the library. As soon as the planting is complete, the Library will erect four small (approximately 12"x15") signs on either side at each end of the planting area, stating "Newly Planted Area, Please Do Not Step Off the Sidewalk." Such signs shall remain or be replaced for the first nine months after the gardens are planted. The Library will acknowledge the gift by an article in the first Library Friends Newsletter mailed after the planting is complete. Within two months after the planting is complete, the Library will host, at its cost, a "tea-party" reception for members of the Women's Club, the Master Gardeners, and the Friends of the Library, at which time an "unveiling" of the newly planted gardens will be celebrated.

The Women's Club will provide funds to purchase the necessary equipment, supplies, and plants for the initial planting of the gardens, such funds to be available by August 1, 2009 (see attached budget). Beginning October 15, 2010, the Women's Club will ensure that the beds are mulched in the spring and fall, weeded when necessary, and plants removed or replaced as necessary. They may, at their discretion, hire this work to be done or may recruit volunteers. The Women's Club will allocate enough money annually from their budget to keep the gardens in excellent condition, as determined by the Library Gardens Committee.

The Master Gardeners will prepare the new beds, will undertake such soil amendment as necessary, will install a drip irrigation system on a timer, and will purchase plants and plant them in the new gardens. This work will be complete by October 15, 2009. The MGs will also check the gardens weekly during the first year (October 15, 2009 – October 14, 2010), insuring that the plants are thriving, removing weeds and debris, and checking that the drip irrigation system is operating properly. During the first year, the MGs will turn off the irrigation system in the fall and restart it in the spring.

The Library Gardens Committee will consist of two members each from the Women's Club, the Master Gardeners, and the Library Friends. All members will be appointed by their respective organizations for a term of three years, and may be reappointed for one additional three-year term. The director of the Library will sit on this committee ex officio. The Library Gardens Committee will oversee the maintenance of the gardens and will report in writing to their respective organizations quarterly. The Library Gardens Committee may, at its discretion, recommend at any time that the garden program be discontinued.

Any party to this agreement that decides to withdraw from the agreement must give all other parties at least 180 days' notice.

Any disputes that arise regarding the new gardens will be arbitrated by a panel consisting of the presidents of the Women's Club and the Library Friends, together with the Mayor of Anywhere.

Signed:

_____   Date _____

President, The Women's Club of Anywhere

_____   Date _____

President, The Friends of the Library

_____   Date _____

Representing the Master Gardeners

_____   Date _____

Director, Library of Anywhere

Summary

Picking a goal—the problem to be solved—can often be quite simple once we understand the problem. Phrasing the goal as a "We will . . ." sentence clearly identifies what we expect to accomplish and what the result will look like. Deciding how to accomplish the goal is the question.

We usually have several alternative paths to our goal. Deciding which of those programs to undertake requires a realistic look at the resources we have available and the time we have to complete the program.

We will want to be sure we have carefully thought out our budget and have prepared a rudimentary cash-flow analysis. We will want to be sure we have selected the right partners to work with us. To be sure that we all understand our roles, we will each sign a Memorandum of Understanding that clearly spells out each partner's responsibilities.

Evaluation

I n Chapter 5 we are going to look at the importance of a formal evaluation strategy in order to monitor your program's progress. We are going to examine the components of a good evaluation plan. Finally, we are going to remind ourselves of the benefits to be gained for future programming when we have a written comprehensive evaluation summary of the completed project.

As your program nears completion, you'll probably begin to think of planning a celebration with your partners. You will want to salute all those who have made this achievement possible. If you don't, you are missing a wonderful opportunity to thank those who worked with you to make this program successful.

But you should never assume, just from appearances, that your goal has been met, nor that it has been met in the most effective way. Sure, you know what people tell you. They may be singing your praises. They may be telling others about your wonderful work. They may have offered you reports describing the benefits received because of your work.

When dealing with officials of the Soviet Union, President Ronald Reagan often quoted a translation of a Russian proverb, "Trust, but verify." This is good advice for any of us implementing any kind of change program. Remember, if we ask people how they think the project went, people will usually tell us what they think we want to hear. So we can't rely on just what people tell us. Nor in most cases can we rely on a casual observation of the final result. We need to know more than meets the eye.

That's why we need to set up for a program of evaluation even before we start the project. We need to determine just what we accomplished, and at what cost. Remember, we need to "verify."

Setting up a formal approach to evaluation before we even get started with the project may seem like over-kill. In the preceding chapters we've already gone through the entire process of looking at our choices and making our decision. We know what we want to do, how, with whom, when, and where. Why do we need to set up yet another process—one that we won't even use until the program is ended, or at least is well on its way? Isn't this just a bit too much?

No, it isn't. Establishing a simple evaluation process now will keep you on track, will ensure that you use your resources more wisely, and will give you detailed information should you choose to replicate a successful program. You will want to decide before you start what you are going to want to measure. Then you'll be able to collect the right information along the way.

Actually, an evaluation process is really a simple matter, as you'll see shortly.

For too long we have approached "good works" as though the intent is the only important thing. But remember the old saying: The road to Hell is paved with good intentions. "Intentions" don't solve problems. "Intentions" don't feed hungry people, house the homeless, or treat the sick. Intentions are good insofar as they get us moving, get us started on something. But intentions alone have never solved a single problem in the world.

So although we need to start our program with our good intentions, we need to end our program with a good evaluation.

What are the components of that good evaluation? Actually, they are exactly the same questions that you'd ask anyhow!

You start with the goal, just as you did in your MOU. Did we meet our goal? The simple answer to the question is just yes, or no. If you have stated your goal clearly, you should be able to answer this question clearly.

If your answer is yes, congratulations are in order. You have tackled a problem and solved it. The world is a better place because of your work.

Whether the problem you solved was large or small, it was of great importance to someone, and you have done a good deed.

We can always hope the answer will be a clear "Yes." Sometimes, however, the answer is "No." If that's your answer, that's OK too. So you didn't meet your goal. Nevertheless, you undoubtedly accomplished some good, if not the amount of good that you anticipated. Regardless, you probably learned a great deal that will enable you to do a better job next time.

In most cases the answer is going to be, "Well, almost." Goals are elusive things. As careful as we are to state our goal carefully—to limit it to just exactly what we want to accomplish—we usually find that the goal mutates into something a bit different along the way. That's OK if the change turns the goal into something better. If the goal slithers into something less effective, you need to take immediate corrective action right away.

So you will want to know if you hit the mark. Did your program do what it intended? Who benefitted? What was the benefit? Was it what you expected? Did it fix the problem? Did it have unexpected additional benefits? For whom? What were they?

Next, you will want to know if you used the right activities and the right resources. Should you have done other things? What things? Should you have arranged your activities in a different order? Did you start activities that later turned out to be unnecessary, or even dead ends? Did they waste resources?

Were you missing key resources? Did the partnership work out the way you expected? How about timing: Did this take longer than you expected? What activities were most time-consuming?

As you can see, none of these questions are tricky. These questions are those that any prudent person would ask.

Assuredly, your partners will want to know whether the program was a success, and why. Especially any "silent" partners, such as donors, will want to know that their resources were used in a responsible and effective manner.

Of course, you have to collect information in order to complete your evaluation. The best way is to start with "base-line" information (documenting the condition or situation before you begin the program). If you are going to improve SAT scores in your local high school, you'll need to document the current scores. That information should be readily available. But sometimes the information doesn't already exist. Then you'll have to use questionnaires or conduct interviews. Sometimes photos are good documentation (take pictures of that playground before you make any changes). You will probably want to use a combination of these ways anyhow, as you seek to obtain permission to undertake the program, or to invite others into partnership with you.

Then collect information during the program implementation. Take more pictures. Talk with the beneficiaries to get their opinion of progress being made.

Be careful that you do not inadvertently fall into one of the fables that persist in the international development field. Far too often we hear, "People in poorer parts of the world cannot write reports like we do, or manage budgets, or live up to our accountability standards."

Sure they can. People everywhere are smart. In fact, if you think about it, maybe it takes a lot more "smarts" to survive in some of the poorest parts of the world than it does in our own neighborhoods.

Just because some of our partners may not be familiar with our methods doesn't mean that they can't learn them and apply them. Probably all they need is some instruction. And teaching someone how to prepare a budget that meets our expectations prepares that person to be able to meet this expectation when other programs come up. This educational component may well be another benefit of our planned program.

We should hold everyone accountable—ourselves, and all our partners— no matter what our background or education. Of course, we would not expect someone to already have a particular technical skill. We wouldn't expect a person with an eighth-grade education to be a rocket-scientist (to stretch a point). But we would expect that person to be aware of the conditions in his or her home village that might affect the outcome of our project.

So we hold all of our partners accountable, anticipating that they will live up to our expectations—or we build into our program an educational component to give them the skills they will need.

So all partners need to keep careful records, especially financial records and records of donated services and goods. Then you will have all the information you need for the final evaluation.

The following is an example of a how a program-end evaluation might be put together. Reading through it will give you a good idea of how an evaluation might look.

The Program Goal

A good evaluation program starts with a clear description of the intended goal. You learned how to do that in Chapter 4, Decision. You wrote a one-sentence statement of your goal—the result you intended. Remember, that result was designed to be the solution to the problem. The goal cannot simply be an activity toward an eventual solution. You may be able to solve only one part of a larger problem, but you need to isolate your part and identify it.

Some very large programs will have component goals. Let's take as an example wiping out malaria in sub-Saharan Africa. That's a *huge* goal but one with enormous ramifications for the well-being of billions of people.

Authorities estimate that each year there are more than five hundred million cases of malaria around the world. Well over a million people die, most of them young children—and most of these deaths are in sub-Sahara Africa.

People living in poverty are more at risk of contracting malaria, because of lack of adequate shelter and preventive measures, but malaria is also a major cause of poverty. Adults suffering from malaria are frequently unable to work—whether on their own farm plots or in local industries. A large population suffering from malaria is certain to hinder any kind of economic development.

The problem is malaria is so widespread and so complicated that it is unlikely to be solved quickly. No vaccine yet exists. No cure yet exists. Drugs that control its symptoms are available in first-world countries, and in cities in Africa, but generally are not available in the more remote regions of sub-Sahara Africa.

Many, many people are working diligently on this problem. Entire non-profit organizations are dedicated to eradication of malaria. Much research is going into ways to combat it. But there is still a lot of room for individuals or small groups to be involved. Preventing individual cases of malaria is easy and very low cost.

For one thing, the Anopheles mosquito (the malaria carrier) usually is active only between midnight and four a.m. Those pesky mosquitoes biting at dusk may be annoying and may create very itchy bumps, but they don't transmit malaria.

So think: What are most people, particularly children (the most susceptible to the serious consequences of malaria) doing during those hours? Sleeping, of course. How can we prevent their getting malaria? Being sure that they won't get bitten. How to do that? Easy. Cover their beds with bed nets. Bed nets are cheap, long lasting, and very effective. Bed nets have proved to be eighty percent effective in preventing bitcs from malaria mosquitoes.

Even better, if we can provide bed nets impregnated with an insecticide that is safe for children but deadly for mosquitoes, we'll eradicate any mosquitoes silly enough to land on the bed net (and they will, attracted by the children sleeping under it). Slowly, over time, we'll reduce the number of mosquitoes (the only ones carrying the malaria parasite are females, so we'll prevent their producing more mosquitoes).

If we could get every family in a village sleeping under a bed net, we would rapidly reduce the mosquito population in that village and the immediate surrounding area.

How much does a bed net cost? A few dollars, plus the cost of transportation and educating the populace in its use (for example, most nets can be washed, but should not be dried in the sun, which reduces the potency of the insecticide).

An individual could have a goal to prevent the children in only one family from contracting malaria, by contributing money for one bed net.

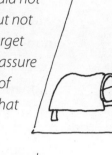

> ◦◦ *But a small development organization decided to take as its goal the elimination of malaria in an entire village by "covering" all the beds in that village with mosquito nets. The group knew it could not carry out this program by itself—it had money for the nets, but not enough money or other resources to personally choose the target village, deliver the nets, educate the villagers in their use, and assure their compliance. So the group decided to work through one of the organizations set up to facilitate this work, but knowing that it would have a real stake in the organization's success.*
>
> *So, taking this example, the group set as its goal a portion of a much larger goal—knowing that it would have real impact—perhaps a life and death impact—on someone's life.* ◦◦

The group set out to raise two thousand five hundred dollars, which would underwrite the cost of approximately one hundred mosquito nets, including delivery and education. Unfortunately, they raised only two thousand dollars. So, did they meet their component of the overall goal? Did they accomplish what they set out to do?

In this case, they missed the mark. They got only eighty percent of the way there. Does this mean that the project to protect all the people in the village failed? Well, yes, and no. On their own, the group did not meet one hundred percent of their goal. But remember the story of the starfish? The program made a difference to all of the children who were now protected from mosquito bites as they slept. For them, the project was one hundred percent effective. The only ones who did not benefit were the remaining twenty percent.

This is where partnership is valuable. Fortunately, the implementing organization was able to shift some of its resources to make up the difference. So all the village homes received bed nets.

The overall project was a success, but our illustrative group did not achieve its goal. Should it have examined its fundraising activities midstream when funds were slow in arriving? Should it have tried a different approach to fundraising? Where could it have taken corrective action? These are all questions that the evaluators should answer.

Let's look at one more example:

> ෨ *Another group's goal was to maintain the good health of the senior citizens in its community by encouraging each one to be vaccinated against pneumonia. They knew at the outset that they would not be able to vaccinate everyone. Some people would not be willing to be vaccinated, some might have religious objections, and some will simply slip through that old proverbial crack. But in setting up their goal, the group knew approximately how many seniors lived in their community, and could count how many vaccinations were given, so they could easily establish a target "penetration" rate (an apt word when describing shots, no?). Their objective was to reach ninety-five percent of the eligible seniors.*
>
> *At the conclusion of the program, the group gave more vaccinations than the number of senior citizens they had thought lived in their town. Either they miscounted to begin with, or the program attracted "visitors" from neighboring towns. Either way, they obviously accomplished their objective.* ෨

So the simple answer to the question is just yes, or no. If you have clearly stated your goal, you should be able to clearly answer this question.

Part of the evaluation of the goal is to describe what enabled you to hit the mark, or what prevented you from achieving it. Memories are short. In a few years, another group may want to try the same program. Your notes will be invaluable for them. Save your findings for posterity.

The Resources Used

A good evaluation document carefully lists all resources used in the program. Remember that the term "resources" doesn't mean just money. It means donated supplies and services, volunteer time, expertise.

If money was spent, the evaluation must include a full financial accounting. That document must show all sources of funds (contributions, revenues from money-making projects, grants from foundations or governments) and all expenditures by type (materials, salaries, permits, travel, etc.). Good project management includes keeping complete records, so this information should be pretty easy to summarize.

If materials were donated, evaluators should find a way to put a value on those materials. Your local lumberyard can tell you the value of donated lumber. Your local paint store can tell you what a can of paint would have cost. Even the value of donated space can be calculated using local rental rates.

Anyone who uses a car for transportation directly related to the program should estimate the mileage, and that resource should be calculated using the current government-allowed reimbursement rate.

Non-monetary or intangible donations are, admittedly, harder to value. Frequently we think, "Ah, well, counting those isn't really important." But it is, for two reasons:

First, those who contribute money to your program like to see their investment "leveraged" by donations of time, talent, and goods. If you can show that you got eight dollars of value for every dollar that was donated in cash, your donors will be delighted, and many of them will be more inclined to contribute to your next venture.

Second, you need to know exactly what your total program cost was. At some point you are going to want to do what is called a cost-benefit analysis. If you don't put a value on those non-monetary inputs, you won't know what your program really cost. Imagine that someone reads about a project you just completed, and learns that it "cost" only one hundred dollars (the cash contribution). They decide to do the same program with their hundred dollars, only to find that they don't have nearly enough money. They didn't know that you had a thousand dollars worth of non-cash contributions that made up the bulk of your resources. You will have inadvertently misled them by not being scrupulous in your valuation of non-cash contributions.

A common mistake project managers make is to allow someone to pay for some resource or service, and then refuse to be reimbursed for the expense. The "generous donor" says, "I don't want to be repaid; just consider it a contribution." The danger here is that if you don't enter the expenditure on your books, then you do not have complete records of the actual cost of your program. If you don't count it, you will never know what your project really cost. Your evaluation will be skewed, and those who later try to duplicate your program will be in for some nasty surprises. They will underestimate the cost of the next program because of these hidden donations.

If you are faced with this situation, ask the donor to let you reimburse them and then, if they want to, they can make a cash donation to the organization in the same amount. This keeps the records straight.

An example: Because of extremely busy daytime schedules, your leadership group meets once a month over a modest dinner at a local restaurant. The organization has a policy to pay for the dinner, in part to thank those giving of their time (their resource) to the program.

If one member decides to be extraordinarily generous and picks up the tab one month, the accounts of the program will show less expense for the board meetings. Should the organization want to repeat the program some years later, having forgotten the generous gesture, they will underestimate the cost of the leadership dinners.

So you must put a value on all resources, whether monetary or not, in order to come up with a valid evaluation.

If volunteers donated time, you should have a system for valuing that resource. A simple way is to just keep track of the number of hours donated and multiply that times the minimum wage. This will give you a really conservative figure, but one that can easily be defended as the minimum value of that input.

If your project requires the skills of professionals, you should increase the value of the donated services by using a more appropriate measurement. For example, a program to enable volunteer pediatricians to provide free well-baby evaluations in low-income areas should calculate the value of the medical services at a much higher per-hour rate.

You may want to track contributed services by category. However you do so, please do track them. You'll find that calculation becomes important—people will be amazed at the forces you've been able to put to work. And those who donate money will be delighted to see their dollars enhanced by the additional non-monetary resources.

Your partners are also resources. How did each partnership work out? Did you need other, or more, partners? What went smoothly? What got bumpy? Were your partners satisfied? (Each partner should do his or her own evaluation and ideally share the results with all other partners.)

The Activities Accomplished

What did you *do*? (This is not the place to look at whether you met your goal—this is the time to look at each activity that you engaged in to get you to your goal.) How did you employ your resources? Which activities "cost" the most? Which were most productive, and which were, ultimately, a waste of time? These are thought-provoking questions and can't be answered quickly. They require some reflection, and even some information gathering from our partners. What activities would you have done differently? What have you learned?

The Timeline

How accurate was your estimate of the time this project would take? Did it go more quickly than you anticipated (rare, but sometimes happens)? Did it take longer (more likely)? One corollary of Murphy's Law says: However long it is going to take, it takes longer. That is unfortunately more likely to be true in this kind of work.

What part of the project went according to the planned timeline? Where were the delays? What caused them? How could they have been prevented? What additional problems did the delays create? Did you move too quickly in any area? Where were you able to speed up the process?

The Partnership

With whom did you partner? Were these the right partners? What did each partner contribute? What agreement did you have with each partner? Were the agreements in writing (in other words, did you create an MOU)? Were the agreements well constructed or did you discover gaps? Did each partner live up to the agreement? If not, why not? Were there any misunderstandings? How could they have been avoided? What went particularly well? Which partners would you work with again? Which partner would you avoid if you were to do another program?

The Cost/Benefit Analysis

OK, you achieved your goal, but at what cost? Let's assume that your goal was to ensure that high school graduates in your town had sufficient computer skills to be eligible for entry-level jobs. Let's say that the program cost one thousand dollars, and all one hundred of this year's graduates now have the requisite computer skills. The cost per student is ten dollars.

If the program resulted in only ten capable students, the cost would escalate to one hundred dollars per student. As you evaluate whether or not to continue this program, you might find that the benefits per student for this particular program just do not justify the cost. You might want to explore some other program that produces more benefit per dollar spent.

In order to measure some of these elements, you may have to develop surveys, or interviews, or research public information such as SAT scores. You may have to develop your own measurement tools, specific to your project. If you are in a quandary about how to go about this, see if you can't find a volunteer who has some expertise in this area. Surveys, in particular, can be tricky—get the best advice you can before you embark on one.

Findings

Up to this point, we've been employing quite objective measurements. In most cases, we have a clear choice between yes and no, or we can add up the dollars spent, calculate the number of hours of volunteer time, or document the materials consumed.

So now you need to reflect. What did you learn? What did you learn about goal setting? About estimating necessary resources? About partnerships? About how to implement a program? We could even ask: What did you learn about how to conduct an evaluation?

Take some time with this portion of the evaluation. Think about what you learned, and think about it again tomorrow. Discuss your findings with your partners. Discuss your findings with others who were not directly involved, but who knew about the program.

Conclusion

Here is where you get to summarize the most important points of the evaluation. You may want to write two or even three conclusions, depending upon the audience. Your might write one conclusion to a foundation donor, which would feature how you used its grant; a different version (same conclusion, but different focus) to your beneficiary partner, reviewing what you have accomplished together as partners; and a third to report to your organization's board of directors, who are going to be interested in the cost-benefit analysis and recommendations for making your organization's input more effective in future programs. All of these conclusions will be true and accurate; they will differ only in emphasis. All of those to whom you report will want to examine your findings to guide them when making decisions on new programs in the future.

Evaluation isn't difficult, it isn't time-consuming, but it does need to be done if we are to learn from our triumphs and our mistakes. Outreach is a learning experience for all of us who do it, and we will get better and better at it if we evaluate each of our efforts.

Summary

Evaluation is a necessary part of any program. Planning for the evaluation gives management the tools to monitor program progress. Program-end evaluation describes what happened, at what cost, with what successes and difficulties. It provides a brief overview of the activities of the project, the resources used, the input of the partners. It also provides a guide for future programming.

Familiarity Breeds Success

Remember *Pygmalion* (or *My Fair Lady*)? Remember Henry Higgins exclaiming "By Jove, she's got it!" when Eliza finally spoke "The rain in Spain falls mainly in the plain" in a rolling, proper, upper-class English accent? Remember the jubilation?

Well, by Jove, *you've got it*! You are familiar with all aspects of the better way of doing good. And with that familiarity, you'll be well on your way to success!

You've learned to be cautious, but sure of what you want to achieve. You've seen the wisdom of reducing your goal to one simple sentence. You've counted the myriad resources you have at hand. You've examined various alternative activities you might undertake to achieve your goal. You know the importance of including partners in your work and preparing MOUs with them.

You are comfortable preparing budgets, cash-flow and work-flow charts, and timelines. You know the pitfalls of unintended consequences. And you are on the lookout for old Murphy's Law.

You know you can work at home or abroad. You know you can come up with brilliant new ideas or execute someone else's great idea. You know you have to anticipate delays and pleasant surprises. You know you'll encounter resistance. And you know when you prepare your project-end evaluation, you'll probably wow those who thought your plan wouldn't work (because it undoubtedly will if you just follow the process presented in this book).

Just to show you how much you have learned, take a few moments and answer the following questions. You'll zip through them with confidence. You'll realize that you are now a qualified practitioner of Doing Good the Better Way.

Potential Program Checklist

1. In what particular geographic region or program sector do you want to work? Why?

2. Have you investigated other regions or sectors?

3. How did you choose this program?

4. Who is advocating for this project, and why?

5. Who are the local stakeholders?

6. Have all stakeholders been invited to participate?

7. Who else is addressing needs in this area or sector? Have you talked with them to understand their program and goal?

8. Do you have the capacity to undertake this program?

9. Should you enter into this program (ethically, morally, etc.)?

10. Who are the potential program partners? Are they:
    a. Credible
    b. Reliable
    c. Capable
    d. Accountable?

11. How do you know?

12. Is the program culturally acceptable?

13. What could go wrong?

14. Can you summarize your prospective program in one written document, including:
    a. What is to be achieved?
    b. When?
    c. How will it be achieved?
    d. How will it be measured?
    e. When?
    f. What are the commitments of each participating party?
    g. Who is responsible for what?
    h. When will payments be made?
    i. When will reports be due?

I am willing to wager you just waltzed through the questions above, knowing that you have learned every step in this Outreach approach. You now can be confident that you understand "The Better Way of Doing Good." So get on with it.

And good luck!

∽

Author's Note

I'd love to know your successes, and if you have questions or problems, I'll like to know those too. I'll do the best I can to assist you. After all, now that you've learned "The Better Way of Doing Good," we're Partners, aren't we?

You can reach me at **betterwayofdoinggood@yahoo.com.**

For Further Reading

The following books are those I have found most helpful in developing my understanding of "the better way of doing good."

Alkire, Sabine, and Edmund Newell. *What Can One Person Do?: Faith to Heal a Broken World*. New York: Church Publishing Incorporated, 2005. A discussion of the Millennium Development Goals and how individuals or small groups can participate in their achievement.

Black, Maggie. *The No-Nonsense Guide to International Development*. Oxford: New Internationalists Publications Ltd., 2003. A short introduction to the world of development – its potential and its practices, some brilliant and effective, others treacherous and fraudulent.

Brest, Paul, and Hal Harvey. *Money Well Spent: A Strategic Plan for Smart Philanthropy*. New York: Bloomberg Press, 2008. A handbook for donors, demonstrating that the size of the gift is not so important as developing a strategy for using it successfully.

Collier, Paul. *The Bottom Billion: Why the Poorest Countries Are Failing and What Can Be Done About It*. New York: Oxford University Press, 2007. A clear-eyed look at the remaining pockets of unrelenting poverty in the world and why overcoming them has proved so difficult.

Crutchfield, Leslie R., and Heather McLeod Grant. *Forces for Good: The Six Practices of High-Impact Nonprofits*. San Francisco: Jossey-Bass, 2008. Excellent information for evaluating potential program partners or possible recipients of donations or grants.

Drucker, Peter F. *Managing in a Time of Great Change*. New York: Truman Talley Books/Dutton, 1995. Philanthropy's goal is transformation for good. This book provides a fresh look at new methods of managing the sometimes tricky aspects of change.

Easterly, William. *The White Man's Burden*. New York: The Penguin Press, 2006. A provocative look at the (lack of) results of foreign aid to help the world's poorest people.

Edwards, Michael, and Alan Fowler, eds. *The Earthscan Reader on NGO Management*. London: Earthscan Publications Ltd., 2002. A detailed look at how nonprofits can improve their management, programs, and results.

Fairbanks, Michael, and Stace Lindsay. *Plowing the Sea: Nurturing the Hidden Sources of Growth in the Developing World*. Boston: Harvard Business School Press, 1997. The new models for business development in the developing world provide strategies for those dedicated to elimination of poverty and inequality.

Firstenberg, Paul B. *Managing for Profit in the Nonprofit World*. New York: The Foundation Center, 1986. A tried-and-true discussion of management techniques that result in better nonprofit program delivery and more efficient administration.

Friedman, Thomas L. *Hot, Flat, and Crowded*. New York: Farrar, Straus and Giroux, 2008. A sobering look at world demographic trends and their implications for global sustainability. A good primer for those interested in international development programs.

Frumkin, Peter. *Strategic Giving: The Art and Science of Philanthropy*. Chicago and London: The University of Chicago Press, 2006. Written for the potential donor, this book challenges nonprofits and their funders to adopt better models of accountability.

Gary, Tracy, with Nancy Adess. *Inspired Philanthropy* (3rd ed.). San Francisco: Jossey-Bass, 2008. As the subtitle says, "Your Step-by-Step Guide to Creating a Giving Plan and Leaving a Legacy."

Harrison, Lawrence E., and Samuel P. Huntington, eds. *Culture Matters: How Values Shape Human Progress*. New York: Basic Books, 2000. Understanding cultural differences can make or break a development program addressing poverty and injustice.

Kaplan, Robert S., and David P. Norton. *The Strategy-Focused Organization: How Balanced Scorecard Companies Thrive in the New Business Environment*. Boston: Harvard Business School Press, 2001. Excellent advice for nonprofit organizations that want to be more effective change-agents.

Kinsolver, Barbara. *The Poisonwood Bible*. New York: HarperPerennial, 1999. This novel accurately portrays the tragedy of ill-conceived do-good programs carried out by persons with no awareness of different cultural, political, or religious realities.

Kotler, Philip, and Alan R. Andreasen. *Strategic Marketing for NonProfit Organizations*. Upper Saddle River, NJ: Prentice Hall, 1996. Good intentions must be translated into good outcomes. Marketing is an under-utilized tool in nonprofit programming that can create lasting impact.

Micklethwait, John, and Adrian Wooldridge. *A Future Perfect: The Challenge and Hidden Promise of Globalization*. New York: Crown Business, 2000. An interesting look at how globalization, which is here to stay, may impact the lives of us all, no matter where we live or work.

Sachs, Jeffrey. *The End of Poverty: Economic Possibilities for Our Time*. New York: The Penguin Press, 2005. A book both highly praised and highly criticized, it should be read for its perspective on world development issues and the author's prescription for progress.

Theroux, Paul. *Dark Star Safari: Overland from Cairo to Capetown*. Wilmington, MA: Mariner Books, 2003. A renowned travel writer's dark perspective on the ineffectiveness of forty years of foreign aid in Africa. A sobering look at the "business" of development.

Tyler Scott, Katherine. *Creating Caring & Capable Boards: Reclaiming the Passion for Active Trusteeship*. San Francisco: Jossey-Bass Publishers, 2000. Provides not-for-profit organizations with a new framework for effective governance. ·

Yunus, Muhammad. *Creating a World Without Poverty: Social Business and the Future of Capitalism*. New York: Public Affairs, 2007. Nobel Peace Prize-winner Yunus founded Grameen Bank, the first micro-credit program, and now calls for expanded ways to use business methods to confront social issues.

Zakaria, Fareed. *The Future of Freedom: Illiberal Democracy at Home and Abroad*. New York and London: W. W. Norton & Company, 2004. Understanding the influence of differing political systems is critical to implementing major development programs. This book presents a clear picture of current political realities worldwide.